M000219768

Do Not Discard

Do Not Discard

The Story of Sam

*Based on the true story of
a baby boy, discovered in the trash,
who goes on to triumph with
the help of ordinary people.*

MARLENE BYRNE

First Edition 2023.
Published by Good Stories Publishing LLC
Copyright © Good Stories Publishing LLC 2023

Library of Congress Control Number: 2022917751
Library of Congress Cataloging-in-Publication Data

DO NOT DISCARD
By Marlene Byrne
ISBN: 978-1-7370092-2-1

Website: www.marlenebyrne.com
Editing: Heather Pendley/David Haznaw
Cover and book design: Tamian Wood, www.BeyondDesignBooks.com

Based on a true story. Some names have been changed. Some stories have been enhanced.

Dedication

"One man's trash is another man's treasure."

This book is dedicated to Samuel,
a true treasure to everyone he meets.

Table of Contents

Foreword
Step into the World of Sam

As you read this book, you might catch yourself asking, "Is this story *really* true, or has it been embellished for entertainment value?"

Let me assure you that while some of the names have been changed, the story has accurately captured the remarkable and true journey of Sam.

Sam had a traumatic beginning, born to unknown parents with stomach issues and thrown into the trash as a baby. Yet, this is not a story about tragedy. Rather, it's about strength, faith, family, and the tenacity to achieve great things even through hardship.

I met Sam at the *Nuestros Pequeños Hermanos* (NPH) home in El Salvador. The name translates to Our Little Brothers and Sisters and was founded in Mexico in 1954 by Father William Wasson. NPH is an organization that cares for and raises orphaned, abandoned, and at-risk children. From a single orphanage, NPH has grown significantly, and today operates nine homes in Latin America and the Caribbean. The homes not only care for children in each home but reach out beyond the walls of each orphanage to support vulnerable children in the surrounding communities.

In 1989, immediately after graduating from college, I volunteered for one life-changing year at NPH Mexico. Fifteen years later, after having become ordained as a priest in the Archdiocese of Chicago, I returned for a five-year assignment as regional director of NPH Central America, living at the home in El Salvador.

While this book reflects on the astonishing story of one individual, Samuel's spirit of hope and perseverance is reflected in the thousands of children whose lives have been transformed while growing up at NPH. I had the privilege to live and learn from so many of the children at NPH, all of them with stories of hardship, tragedy, and struggle.

One of the many hats I wore at NPH was driver's education teacher. I'm convinced some of the moments in the car are what triggered the first of many gray hairs that now cover my head.

I taught Sam to drive. Like so many of his fellow *pequeños*, he was thrilled to receive his driver's license, and later, to be assigned as my personal driver.

Sam drove me to the airport, into the local town for meetings, and to the supermarket. When I returned to Chicago after my five-year stay in El Salvador, Sam had moved to Chicago and ironically, I began driving him around, most often to a local church that celebrated Mass in Spanish.

As we piled up the miles in a white pickup truck in El Salvador, and later in my humble sedan in Chicago, I got to know Sam and learn about his life journey. Our conversations ran the gamut, from politics to religion, relationships, sports, and occasionally some gossip, or *chisme*. It always impressed me that we could talk about anything, and even when we disagreed, Sam was respectful and always showed interest in understanding my point of view.

One day, while Sam was driving me to the barbershop in Santa Ana, we were debating if NPH did enough to prepare the children for the real world. I insisted that because NPH focused so heavily on education, our children would leave the home and begin their adult lives with skills and degrees that most of their peers could never access.

Sam agreed that NPH did a wonderful job of showering the children with unconditional love, teaching them responsibility, and providing them with a solid education. But he wanted more. He countered with an idea to give the older children who were about to enter the real world training in basic life skills, like how to open a bank account or even how to buy a half-kilo of cheese at the deli counter.

Here's where Sam's unique and beautiful gift presented itself and has remained with me to this day. He never takes life's blessings for granted. Instead of being scarred with bitterness or resentment, he lives with a spirit of pure gratitude, continuously thankful for all he receives. At the same time, he never stops looking to improve the world for those he loves or those who are marginalized, needy, or disadvantaged. Even when he would point out the flaws of NPH or the world in general, he never did so with any guile or resentment. He loved NPH, and thus, would always think of ways to improve it for the current *pequeños* and those who would come after him.

Reflecting on our conversations, I realize Sam has taught me that life is rarely a straight-line journey from point A to point B. Instead, it is filled with twists, turns, accidents, adventures, potholes, unexpected detours, and hopefully, some wonderful surprises along the way.

I thank God for the gift of Sam's friendship and inspiration. I hope you are touched by his improbable, true story. May Sam's extraordinary life inspire you to be filled with hope, peace, and gratitude. More importantly, may it encourage you to help others along the way. It may just be the thing that changes someone's life, and more likely yours, forever.

Most Reverend Ronald A. Hicks
Bishop of Joliet, Illinois

Punch
Jorge

DIEGO GRABBED SAM BY the arm and dragged him outside. Sam's eyes were wide with fear. He knew what would come next. Though he resisted, he was small and not strong enough to stop the force pulling his body toward the door. The seam on his sleeve ripped apart from the tension. Sam fell as Diego pushed open the door. He struggled to get his feet back under his body without tripping on the threshold. The door slammed shut.

Around the corner and out the doorway they went, Diego and Sam, adversaries but not rivals. To me, a rivalry meant both sides had a chance to prevail. That was definitely not the case here.

Victoria and the girls watched too. Stiff. Tense. Scared. They knew better than to step in when Diego was in a rage. Victoria was his obedient wife, and her daughters followed her subservient lead.

Once they were out of sight, Diego took a full swing at Sam's head. Soon, he was beating anything he could; using an open hand on seven-year-old Sam's back, his face, his body, in an attempt to subdue and dominate without leaving any visible evidence.

When Sam finally hit the ground, Diego gave him one last light kick and then relaxed. He was not physically tired, just tired of the act. Knowing he could revisit this situation anytime, he stood tall and walked back to the house without a word.

There are ways to punch a body to avoid leaving marks. Abusers learn quickly that bruises and scratches invite questions from family, friends, and even casual acquaintances. A total stranger will turn their head in judgment and whisper a question to a confidant if they detect signs of abuse. Most will not act, but their opinions will be evident.

Judgment rarely comes from the victim. They keep their thoughts brewing deep inside, as guilt and shame inevitably accompany the physical harm.

The brave ones meet their abuser eye to eye, but that is rare. Sam was just a kid and couldn't stand up to Diego's aggressions. He relied on Diego for everything: food, clothing, shelter, family, and his life.

As Diego's older brother, I was always bigger than him, which curtailed any hostility aimed in my direction. I ignored his verbal taunts. We had completely different personalities. I was like my parents—hard-working, soft-spoken. Diego was like our uncle on Mom's side. Strong. Loud. Some might say a bully. We both knew I was their favorite. How could Diego be? He was constantly doing things to make them angry; getting in trouble with families in the neighborhood and giving our parents cause for angry discussions. "Diego," they would say, "you can't act like this to people." Every conversation would end with an apology and a promise to not behave badly again. Once, I even heard my mother say, "Why can't you be more like your brother, Jorge?"

I remember trying to stop him once when he was hurting another boy. With the boy in a headlock, Diego yelled from the ground, "Jorge, you are too weak and afraid to get what you want!"

I wish I could go back to when we were kids and fight harder to change his aggressive tendencies. But those days are long gone. I watched young Diego's personality grow more violent as he became a teen and then a full-grown adult and part-time predator. In his teens, his confidence turned to arrogance, and in his twenties, as he got stronger, there were more excuses for his behavior. He could let his temper run wild without retribution.

All I could do was watch. I was frozen in place. Not understanding how I could be imperceptible to everyone.

I had wanted nothing more than to be part of Sam's life as he grew up, to see him mature into the man I knew he would be. Stand proud over him as a "father" figure. Instead, I was invisible, watching it unfold.

What started this most recent incident was something most people wouldn't think twice about. Moments earlier, as Sam swept the floor, he bumped a table with the broom, not hard, but just enough to knock a coffee cup to the floor, breaking it.

Diego didn't have patience for what he called stupid mistakes, meaning anything Sam did that wasn't exactly how he ordered it. Diego considered Sam a servant. He wasn't part of the family as he was when he lived with me. To Diego, the boy was a burden, and he rationalized his violent episodes by calling them "teaching moments" that would make Sam a better worker when he was on his own.

For a few minutes after the beating, Sam lay on the porch with his fingers entwined behind his head and his elbows guarding his ears, a posture that helped shield his face and head. He breathed slowly, taking in how his body felt. *It's not too bad this time. Nothing broken. Maybe a bruise on my ribs.* He checked the back of his hands and there was no blood. Ironically, Sam always felt a sense of peace after a beating because it was the only time Diego would leave him alone. He enjoyed peaceful moments by himself with his thoughts before the physical, verbal, and emotional abuse became a threat again.

Diego let the door slam behind him, and it creaked as it bounced one more time before coming to rest. As he entered the living room, Diego stopped to look at the girls and shook his shoulders as if to remove the entire incident from his body, like it was nothing more than dust on his clothes. The girls and Victoria said nothing. They knew better than to make a fuss or have an opinion about Sam. Diego had made it clear that opening their home to him was the only concession he would make, and that Sam was there to work.

This wasn't the first time I had to watch Diego go after Sam. Since his arrival, Sam had suffered a broken rib, a sprained wrist, and bruises on his back. One time, Diego slammed Sam's fingers in a door. A simple punishment was to put Sam in the small room he called a bedroom but was really a closet.

I could tell Sam didn't mind. For him, it was a safe place.

So, when Sam snuck back into the house, he quietly closed the closet door behind him and unrolled a small blanket on the floor. He would go to bed early. For tonight, it gave me relief. But I knew the violence would come again. We all knew. It hurt to know there was absolutely nothing any of us could do about it.

2

Look For Me in the Closet
Sam

THE LITTLE HOLE BETWEEN the woodwork and the closet floor offered promise for my secret project. I had been working on the floorboard for weeks to see if I could get it loose without making noise or leaving any visible marks. It would be a place to safely store money and other treasures. Eventually, I would need them, either when I escaped or when Diego threw me out.

Jorge had taught me how to hide money when we made bread deliveries for the bakery. He was always trying to stay one step ahead of any *banditos* on our route from store to store. He showed me how to remove the sole of my shoe and create a small, secure space, wrapping things in paper so as not to make any noise when I walked. He even gave me coins to practice with.

Diego must have known the shoe trick. Maybe because he and Jorge were brothers. Maybe their father, Alonzo, had taught them. It was hard for me to visualize the three of them together. Alonzo and Jorge seemed similar, but I couldn't understand how Diego was the son of such a kind, caring man. Alonzo's sons were nothing alike and Diego was nothing like his dad.

One day, Diego got the idea that I was stealing from him. He pulled off my shoe and found the coins—my coins. To him, it confirmed his suspicion that I was taking his money.

It was the first time I was hauled out to the garage so Victoria and the girls couldn't hear the beating. I guess Diego thought I might scream or yell. On the way, he pulled a branch off the tree in the backyard to use as a switch, and he unleashed all his anger with it. When it was over, he became extremely calm and sat down on a chair, sweating, staring down at me. He was surprised that I didn't make a sound through the entire beating and, in a way, seemed proud of me for it. What he didn't know was that no matter how much it hurt, I would never give him the satisfaction of crying out. I always held my tongue and took it. No yelling, no pleading. At least my silence didn't make him angrier.

Diego wasn't wrong. I *had* been stealing from him. But he was wrong about the coins in my shoe. Those were mine. I had been grabbing other things when I had the opportunity and securing them in hiding places around the house. I had trinkets hidden under a flat stone near the back porch. I had other treasures wrapped in a cloth, buried under a spout by the corner of the shed.

I even found a way to hide money in the stuffing of a little pillow Victoria had given me. Now that Diego had found my shoe coins, I was desperate to find a better hiding place, something more secure for the long term. That's when I started working on the floorboard in the closet.

As I picked at it, a splinter pierced my finger. The wood was old and dry. The board would come free, but I needed to pry out the nails slowly to prevent it from cracking. The wood had to remain in one piece to be placed back perfectly, undetectable to anyone snooping around in the closet.

I rolled on my back and relaxed, picking at the splinter in my finger. The lighting was bad; a simple, bare bulb hung from the angled ceiling.

In the quiet, I realized how much I missed Jorge. My heart ached for the days riding in his delivery truck and breathing in the wonderful scent of fresh bread. This pain was worse than anything Diego could deliver. I closed my eyes and rubbed the front of my shirt as if it might ease the tightness in my chest.

The day was coming when I would run. But what was out there for me? What was next? I spent my time thinking about how to make my exit, the moment I would run and never look back. I rarely thought about what I was running to. Did anyone who ran away really know where they were headed? Wherever the road took me, I knew it had to be better than this.

There was one item I would take with me, something that would infuriate Diego—a little red toy truck he had placed on a shelf in the living room. Months ago, his sister, Lilian, had sent gifts to the family and included one for me: the truck. Diego decided I didn't deserve the gift. Instead of getting rid of it, he left it sitting there as a reminder to improve my behavior, help more, and move faster when we worked together. There it sat on display for all to see and collect dust, but not for me to play with. I would not be allowed to touch it until he felt my attitude had improved.

I would steal that red truck as a final gesture. I imagined Diego searching for me. I dreamed about how he would comb the streets, driving around town, looking in alleys and parks. He would be steaming mad and yet embarrassed because he would have to tell Alonzo and others that I was gone. I imagined the moment he would finally give up looking for me, when he would stop asking people around the village if they had seen me. The thought of his defeat made me smile.

Once he accepted the fact I was gone, he would return home and sit in his chair. That was the moment it would hit him. He'd look up and see the shelf and realize I had taken that little red truck without his permission.

But it wouldn't end there. I would stop in the garage just before leaving and smash the little red truck with one of his tools, stuffing the broken pieces into his toolbox. It would be his second lesson. He wouldn't open it for a day or two, but when he did, my message would be complete.

Jorge would not have been happy with my plan. "Revenge," he always said, "is the errand of a fool."

Then again, Jorge was no longer here. He couldn't protect me from this life, and nothing from my time with him seemed to matter now.

There was one possession I planned to keep. On one of our delivery trips, Jorge had given me a small, colorfully painted wooden cross with a short chain and little latch. He said people used these to hold keys. Even though I had never owned a key to anything, I treasured it. In fact, the only keys I had ever seen were for Jorge's truck. I loved that keychain and kept it hooked on a small nail at the house. I never worried that Diego would throw it away because, as a devout Catholic, even he would never throw a cross in the trash.

3

Delivering the Bread
Sam

MY MEMORIES OF LIFE with Jorge were vivid. Even though he was gone, his face was imprinted in my mind like one of those events—either joyous or tragic—that freezes in your memory and stays there your whole life. Few moments with Jorge were shocking or noteworthy. We simply lived day by day, working together, with little conversation between us. Yet his face, his actions, and even his smell were clear in my mind.

I saw his forehead, which couldn't disguise his emotions. When he was mad, the lines nestled between his eyebrows would furrow. Those same lines disappeared when he was relaxed or tired. His hands were expressive, but more than that, they showed he was a worker; his palms were dry, wrinkled, and calloused, yet the dark skin on the back of his hands remained smooth and without scars or blemishes. Those hands revealed his deep belief in hard work. He was a man who labored diligently to support his family. And me. And he was proud of it.

Jorge delivered bread. It was important for him to do his job well. He cared for the bread with the same passion and tenderness he had for his family.

I don't remember hearing Jorge ever laugh aloud. Not once. Occasionally, there were smiles and smirks, even a giggle. But he held them for when it really mattered, when he was genuinely happy.

He had a big smile when Camilla was born. I was standing in the doorway with the other two children, and I remember him holding her as he sat in the straight, wooden chair next to the bed where Rosa, his wife, rested. At that moment, with Rosa sleeping next to him and the tiny baby in his arms, he was happy and content. When Camilla arrived, I thought he might want me to leave, but he never did.

I tried to keep the other kids busy while he and Rosa tended to baby Camilla. When I could, I'd steal a glance as they fed her, washed her, and rocked her to sleep; always staying out of the way, making sure I wasn't a nuisance. I wondered if they had held me the same way when I first arrived.

I tried to imagine Rosa's reaction when Jorge walked in the door with a baby he had found while rummaging at the dump. He had told the story of finding me in the trash often.

Hardly able to feed themselves, I wondered what Rosa thought when he brought me through the door. Was she happy? Was he? I never asked. Even today, I never ask a question if I'm afraid of the answer. Jorge didn't like to talk about it anyway. He saw nostalgia as a waste of time. "Hard work and prayer are what's important," he would say.

Jorge had worked hard to get—and keep—his delivery job at the bakery. As his unofficial assistant, I would wait as he went to get the fresh bread from the bakery each morning and drop it at the stops on our route. Once during a rainstorm, I was leaning against the brick wall of the bakery, letting the rain hit my face and chest. The sky was a deep blue with heavy clouds. Far off, over the mountains, the sun was trying to peek through. The rain felt good, better than the feeble showerhead in our backyard that Jorge built for us to shower under, and this water seemed cleaner. I kept an eye on the side door, waiting for it to swing open. When it did, I started to move. I could feel my feet sinking into the mud as I ran toward the truck. Things like water, mud, and storms didn't bother me. One of my favorite senses is feeling cool raindrops falling on my face.

The mud left spotted marks on my legs like the dirt splashes on the wheel flaps of Jorge's rusty old box truck. Jorge yelled at me to get inside, but I wasn't listening.

I ran around back and opened the truck doors wide so Jorge could load the bread. He had covered the batch with a white cloth, soft like a bedsheet but thicker, to protect it from the rain. The loaves were arranged on a large board, stacked in perfect rows, all stuffed into bags. I was never allowed to move the bread and I stood off to the side so as not to bump him or cause an accident. In this down-pour, he was moving quickly.

The rainy season always added an element of fear for the locals. Flash floods and mudslides were common in El Salvador. Without notice, an entire road could be swept away. If that happened, Jorge couldn't deliver the bread, and that was devastating because when you live hand-to-mouth to feed your family, bread must be delivered or you don't get paid.

I loved everything about helping Jorge, from the smell in the truck to the sights along the road. I was happy as we went about our deliveries. Jorge was a serious man, but I loved being around him. He was never cross with me, even when I made a mistake. I realized later that he wasn't particularly nice to me either, but at that point in my life, I had no frame of reference as to what "nice" was. He was stable, dependable, and predictable. And for someone like me, those qualities were enough.

We loaded the truck, slammed the doors, jumped into our seats, and wiped the water from our arms and hair. The rain continued to pour down as we drove away. I remember looking over at Jorge, wondering how he could see the road through the heavy streaks left by the worn-out windshield wipers. Muddy patterns streaked the glass, changing with each swipe. The sound is still clear in my mind; a scratch going one way and a thump on the swipe back. He rarely spoke while driving, and the silence made the *scratch-thump, scratch-thump* of the wipers seem to grow faster and louder with every mile.

After our third stop, we turned toward a mart on the outskirts of town. When we arrived, I ran to the back of the building to hold the doors for Jorge. At seven years old, opening doors was the only thing I could do to help. Jorge would carry the bread and collect the money, like always, and then we would leave.

This place had gas, groceries, and a long rack of candy. Even though I was never allowed to have any, I loved to look at the colorful packages and read the labels. One was caramel, another had nuts. There were colorful sugar candies, including gummies that looked like worms. I wondered, with all the wonderful candy in the world, why anyone would choose to eat worms.

When we returned to the truck, the rain had stopped. That was common. It would rain hard for a bit and then stop, making way for the heat and humidity to set in. We were headed back to town with the windows rolled down, the breeze smelling like rain and only one stop left. Coming over a hill, we saw a car parked diagonally across the road, blocking our path. I wondered if there was a flood in the roadway. Had they run out of gas? Had the car gotten stuck in a rut?

Before I could see what was happening, Jorge yelled at me, "Get down!" I didn't move. "Down on the floor!" he yelled again. It was the last thing he ever said to me.

4

My Green Pouch
Jorge

"DOWN ON THE FLOOR!" I screamed at Sam. I wasn't mad at him but I knew danger was coming.

Sam didn't listen, of course, and he watched the two men approach the truck, one on either side.

I tried to stay calm and talk to the man through my window. The next thing I knew, my door was open and his gun was in my ribs.

"Can I help you?" I asked politely. My hand instinctively went over to Sam's forearm and squeezed.

"Give me your money!" the man yelled.

"Please, we are just poor people. I deliver bread to feed my family," I said, trying to remain calm and not show fear.

"Don't make me ask again!" he yelled.

"Hurry up!" the other man yelled. He was on Sam's side and busy surveying the road.

"Okay. Okay," I replied.

I started to rummage between the seats, among various papers and notes. I had a green zippered pouch and pulled it out from the mess. Taking my time, I opened it, trying to look despondent as I pulled out random bills.

"There has to be more than that!" he screamed. I saw Sam flinch.

"We are just at the start of our route," I argued. "Go look at all the bread in the back."

The green zippered pouch was a decoy. I hoped Sam wouldn't show any surprise as I defended myself. He knew we weren't just starting the route, he also knew I had more money than what was in the pouch.

The man with the gun and I continued arguing about how much money I should have. I stood fast to my claim that this was what I had collected so far.

The argument continued until the man on Sam's side of the car yelled, "We have to go!" His eyes darted from me, then down the road, then to his friend, and finally, back to Sam.

I heard a loud crack and knew at once we were in trouble. There was another loud crack; then boom, boom, boom.

The man on my side took off, back to the little car still blocking the middle of the road. He carried the green pouch tightly in his hand.

I looked at Sam. He rubbed the back of his head and stared at his bloody fingers. He'd been hit. I reached down to put the truck into gear and saw blood dripping down my arm, between my fingers.

Time seemed to stand still as I waited for the men to speed away. Once they were gone, I stomped on the accelerator and drove toward town and the local hospital.

I don't know how I managed to navigate through traffic as we reached town. People were honking and yelling, but I didn't care. I just kept driving. I had to get us to the hospital as fast as possible.

"It will be okay, it will be okay, it will be okay," I said, over and over, like a mantra.

The next thing I remember was my car door opening. I looked back at Sam and saw a man pulling him out of the other side of the truck and carrying him away in his arms. It was chaos when we arrived at the emergency room; people in hospital uniforms racing up to the truck, yelling instructions to one another as some tried to ask questions.

I remember a nurse saying, "This one is bad." Two men quickly pulled me out of the truck and onto a gurney. I felt pressure, but no pain, as they pushed hard on my ribs, trying to stop the bleeding.

As we entered the emergency room, I craned my neck, looking for Sam among all the chaos. Where was he? Was he okay?

I never saw him. The gurney was moving through the emergency room, away from where we'd entered the building. Suddenly, the sounds became muffled and faint. I could tell they were yelling instructions, but everything was in slow motion. I laid back, figuring Sam was gone and focused on each ceiling tile as it passed overhead.

I felt like I was floating. It was pleasant, though I could see doctors and nurses working furiously to save me. A nurse was jabbing my arm to start an IV. A young man grabbed a cart of supplies and was handing bandages to the doctor. Someone had stuck a heart monitor to my chest, and I could hear it beeping. Somewhere, someone yelled to notify surgery that we were coming. From another part of the room, someone called for blood.

I wasn't scared about what would happen to me. I just needed to know Sam was okay.

5

Waking Up
Sam

As I slowly came to, the first thing I noticed was that my head hurt. I opened my eyes and saw Jorge's father, Alonzo, sleeping in a chair across the tiny room. He looked peaceful, so much so it made me believe everything was going to be okay. Alonzo's face was old, but somehow the wrinkles made him look happy. As he slept sitting straight up, he reminded me of Jorge. Still too tired to say anything to him, I let myself drift back to sleep and began dreaming of the day Jorge found me.

"Imagine my surprise," he'd said. "I was at the dump, dropping things on a garbage pile when I noticed something moving. At first, I stepped back, scared, thinking an animal was about to jump out and attack me."

Laughing about it, he continued, "I used a stick to slowly move the trash aside and saw a little hand. Was I imagining this?"

In disbelief and fearful the baby was dead, he slowly pushed the trash away.

"I couldn't believe it when I saw your fingers move again," he told me. "I knelt down and began to dig, uncovering your face and body."

He called me his "garbage dump gift." In one of the dirtiest places on earth, he found me fully dressed and carefully wrapped in a blue blanket.

"It was so filthy I hardly recognized you were a baby," he said.

That morning, falling in and out of sleep for I don't know how long, I continued to have vivid dreams. I was eating candy worms. I was driving the old truck, stretching to reach the pedals. I was sitting on the stoop at Jorge's house.

In one dream, I was riding in the delivery truck holding a baby wrapped in that same blue blanket. At first, the baby's face was familiar and I thought it might be me, but it wasn't. Jorge and I were riding down a bumpy road, and I was holding that tiny baby boy tightly in my lap.

Out the window, I could see a woman standing on the side of the road. She was waving and happy, blowing me a kiss. It was my mother. Wanting to see what she looked like, I pressed my forehead against the window and tried to get a glimpse. There didn't seem to be a face under the scarf that wrapped around her head and draped down her shoulder.

As we drove on, her body became smaller and smaller until she was out of sight. In my dream, I looked over at Jorge. He was happily whistling a song. It was strange since I had never seen him do anything like that. I hoped he would talk to me, but he didn't. He just kept looking straight ahead, as if the baby and I didn't exist.

I looked down at the baby quietly resting in my arms. His dark eyes stared up at me as if he knew I would care for him and keep him safe. He had dirt on his forehead and cheek. I wiped it away. Jorge reached over and began rubbing the baby's forearm, touching it softly, like he was afraid he might hurt him if he pressed too hard.

Again, I woke up, this time trying to understand what the dreams meant. When I opened my eyes, Alonzo was awake, sitting next to my bed, and softly rubbing my arm. He smiled but I could see the worry in his eyes. I took a deep breath and tried to talk, but nothing came out, and again, I drifted off to sleep.

The next time I woke up, it was night. I opened my eyes to a dark, empty room. Something was beeping and there was a rustling of people outside in the hall. I thought about moving, but I hurt everywhere, and it seemed like even moving one muscle was impossible. My head ached so much there was pain with every blink. I let my eyes drift shut again.

6

From Above

Jorge

I FELT CALM AS everything started to fade: the sounds, the lights, the people. I noticed the doctor's shoulders. He looked up at the clock as he started to pull off his gloves. The fight was over, his and mine. "Time of death . . ."

So, this is death. Simple. Quiet. Here.

I contemplated the scene for a time. It was as if I knew these people as they walked around taking care of patients. None of it made sense, yet the realization of life and the world going on long after I was gone seemed clear.

Where was Sammy?

My answer came as I saw the doctor talking to my father, Alonzo. My father was heartbroken, and suddenly, I felt the reality that I would never talk to him again. He turned, with his head hanging low, and walked down the hallway into another hospital room, Sammy's room.

When we arrived at the hospital in my truck, I had no idea how badly Sam was wounded, but there he was, and it was clear he had survived. In the hospital bed, his body looked small and vulnerable. Not the kid who, just hours before, had endless energy on our delivery run.

For hours, my father sat by his side. I could only imagine how he felt, just sitting there, waiting for something—anything—to change.

The long night was the same as when I waited for Camilla to be born. Nothing to do. No way to help. Just waiting.

I spent the next week watching Alonzo go in and out of Sammy's room. First, just sitting or napping next to his bed. Then, once Sam was awake, talking with him. Sam had asked about me, but Alonzo continued to tell him I was in bad shape. I wasn't sure if he just couldn't bring himself to say that I was dead, or if he was putting off the truth until Sammy's physical wounds started to heal.

After two weeks with Alonzo as Sammy's only visitor, Diego showed up. Sam was to be discharged and they finally told him about my passing. Slowly and painfully, Alonzo delivered the news and, as I expected, Sam quietly accepted it, dropping his head and holding back his tears until he couldn't take it any longer.

After a few moments, Diego told Sam he'd be taking him home to live with his family, where Sam could work for him just like he did for me. Sam didn't seem to care. My father looked worried.

The look on his face made me remember an afternoon when Diego and I were young and found a wounded bird. Diego had called me over to see it, and instinctively I wanted to pick it up and nurse it back to health. Diego would not have it. He grabbed the bird and threw it far into the field.

"We can't help this creature," he said, his face as cold as his words.

That evening, I snuck back to the area where I had dropped a stick as a marker. I searched and searched for that little bird. I listened for chirps. I walked the fields back and forth, pushing aside the tall grass, but I never found it. It had either flown away or its mother had taken it back to the nest.

On the day of Sammy's discharge from the hospital, Alonzo showed up early. Not surprisingly, Diego was late. Alonzo was nervous about sending Sammy home with Diego, but he couldn't expect Rosa to support three of her own children and Sammy too. The boy needed to live with a family. For now, Diego's family would have to suffice.

"I have something for you," my father told Sammy as they sat on the edge of the hospital bed awaiting discharge. He removed a small keychain from his pocket. It was the one with the crucifix Sam had hung on the nail at Jorge's house. Alonzo had been spending time with Rosa to help after Jorge's death and noticed it one afternoon as he paced about the house, grieving for his son and the love and laughter that had been part of Rosa and Jorge's life together.

Sam took the little wooden cross in his hands and rubbed it. Jorge had given it to him in the truck on one of their deliveries, saying everyone should carry one to remember that God and the angels are always watching over them.

"It was from Jorge, yes?" Alonzo asked.

"Yes."

"Keep this as a sign that he will always be with you," Alonzo said.

"Thank you for this," Sammy said, holding back tears.

Alonzo promised himself that he would watch over Sam and protect him. In his grief, it was the least he could do for his dead son. The discharge paperwork took time, and as the nurse finished her instructions, Diego walked in, carrying a small T-shirt and a pair of shorts.

"Here's something of yours to wear home," Diego said without emotion as he tossed the clothes onto the bed.

7

An Orphanage
Jorge

SAM HAD RUN. He wanted out. Up the road with no real direction, he turned down one street after another. It didn't take them long to find him.

I wanted to tell him, "Don't run again!" But I knew Sam couldn't hear me.

He was caught, stuffed in the back seat of a strange car, and sat motionless. I knew what he was thinking. His eyes stared out the window, surveying the landscape, looking side to side. He was marking the buildings on the way back to the home, already plotting his next escape by using landmarks to remember the path out.

If I were there, I could talk to him, reach him. Better yet, I could save him.

Sam had no one to protect or guide him. He ran on instinct, doing what he felt he had to do to survive. As soon as the opportunity presented itself, he'd go right back out the door and run again. But back to what?

I remembered Sam arriving at the orphanage with my father. A large woman with a clipboard had checked him in, getting what little information they could provide about his past. As she asked questions, Alonzo looked to Sam, who wouldn't say anything, so he answered.

"My eldest son, who cared for Sammy, died," Alonzo said. "My other son took him in, but it is not a good situation. I am too old to take care of him while I support my eldest's family. Sam needs a better place."

My father was a good man but knew his two sons were different in many ways, even as young boys. In fact, he had discussed his concerns about Diego with me, always asking me to watch over my brother and try to make him better. It bothered me that my father used that word, "better." To me, Diego was not my problem. He had a temper and didn't think before acting. I learned to keep my distance for my own good and Diego's. But my father's talks with me always ended with, "Remember, we are family, and family always supports one another."

When I was killed, my father focused on Rosa and my girls. He knew they would need his help without me there to provide. When Diego offered to take Sam into his home, it seemed like the best solution. It didn't take long, however, for Alonzo to realize that Diego would never treat Sam as a member of his family.

At first, or at least in front of the family, everything seemed fine. Then one day, Alonzo stopped by unannounced to ask Diego for a tool to repair his truck. As Alonzo entered through the back door, he found Diego and Victoria sitting in the tiny kitchen, preoccupied. When he heard the door slam, Diego jumped up. He was nervous, and before Alonzo could greet him, Diego suggested they go outside. Alonzo recognized the panic in both Diego and Victoria. She remained seated, avoiding eye contact.

As Diego worked his way toward the back door, something made Alonzo stop. He heard a sound coming from the hallway closet. Puzzled, he looked from Diego to Victoria to the door. The tension was thick. In his gut, my father knew what—or to be more exact, who—was in that closet. He slowly walked down the hallway. Diego tried to stop him, but the look Alonzo shot him was clear. There would be no opposing the patriarch of the family.

Alonzo opened the closet door and looked into the deep brown eyes of Sam sitting on the floor against the wall. Sam's look of fear changed to relief when he saw who it was. Alonzo's face, however, went from tension to anger as he looked back at Diego and Victoria.

"What is this?" he yelled.

Nervously, Diego started to speak. "He is being punished for bad behavior." He tried to explain the actions that had precipitated the events, but Alonzo wasn't listening. He held up his hand and the room went silent.

Though Diego's explanation was shallow, Alonzo didn't want to jump to conclusions. His gut told him it was a bigger issue than just this one incident. He started contemplating ways to correct the situation.

He turned to Diego and Victoria. "I am sure this was just for a short time, and now he can come out," he said slowly and quietly as his anger simmered just below the surface. "This will *never* happen again, right?"

Diego nodded and Victoria lowered her head in shame. She couldn't face my father or Sam.

As he drove away, I knew my father felt guilty for being so preoccupied with my death and how it had affected Rosa and the girls. He never thought about how it changed life for Sam. How had he felt losing me? How was he coping with the transition to living with Diego's family? Was he acting out, as Diego explained? Would he resist Diego's punishments or mistreatments? And what would be the punishment if he did?

My father's feeling of dread grew. It's that feeling when you know something to be true but don't want to believe it. He had neglected Sam, which he knew would have disappointed me. He thought about his own feelings for Sam. Was he a grandson or just a kid in their lives? He wasn't sure.

Even if Sam wasn't blood, my father felt a deep sense of right and wrong. Sam living in a closet was wrong, and he would not stand for it.

Two weeks later, my father decided it was time for a second surprise visit. He chose a time when Diego would be working at the market and Victoria would be home alone. It would give him a chance to talk with her and get a better sense of what was happening.

He knocked and Victoria opened the door slightly, peeking out as she held onto the knob. She saw who it was and smiled while still giving the impression he was not welcome inside.

"What can I do for you?" she asked.

"I came to talk," he replied.

"Diego is out," she said. "He won't be home for a few hours."

"I didn't come for him, I came for you," he said as he pushed his way into the house.

She moved aside and closed the door behind them so slowly that it creaked louder than her reply. "For me?"

Father assumed that Diego didn't ask for her opinion on most things. Victoria, he believed correctly, was an obedient wife.

"I see you're cooking," he said, wanting to ease into the conversation with friendly small talk. Victoria didn't take the bait. Instead, she stood stone cold at the end of the kitchen table.

Father walked to the closet and opened the door. On the floor was Sam's blanket, the one he had been lying on just weeks ago. Unfortunately, he wasn't surprised. He looked back at Victoria as the back door opened.

There was Sam, carrying a bucket. He stopped in his tracks and looked down, slowly setting the bucket on the floor.

Father looked puzzled. Sam was typically happy to see him. He walked up to the boy and grabbed his chin and lifted Sam's head. The bruising was undeniable. Both Victoria and Sam stood frozen and afraid.

Father knew the answer but asked anyway. "Sam, how did this happen?"

Sam shrugged so Father asked, "Victoria, do you know where Sam got these bruises?"

She said nothing. Father fixed his gaze on her. "Sam, get your things," he said quietly, but with a level of gravity that made the entire room heavy. Victoria began to cry.

I was so happy at that moment. The man I had respected all my life was doing the thing I wanted most. He was saving Sam from my brother.

Sam did as he was told. He always did. I had tried to instill confidence in him when we were together, but it all seemed lost now. He went to the closet, closed the door for a minute, and reappeared with the blanket rolled in a ball. It wasn't obvious what he had wrapped inside, but it was everything he owned. He stood silently, waiting for Father to make the next move.

As they headed toward the door, Victoria stepped forward to say something but decided against it. She knew the arguing would come when Diego returned. He would want to know that she had fought my father, and she would rather lie to Diego than argue with Alonzo.

Two weeks later, the blanket ball was back in Sam's lap as he rode silently in my father's truck. I had hoped my father might find a way to keep Sam with him, but it was too much. He was old and already caring for my wife and daughters. Money was an issue; there just wasn't enough to go around. Sam couldn't stay, but Father also knew he could not go back to live with Diego.

The orphanage was the next best solution. It was run by the state and while it did not have a good reputation, at least Sam would be cared for and not on the streets like so many other children.

During the trip, Father and Sam did not speak. There was nothing more to say. Sam understood and he liked my father. He knew there wasn't enough space or money. He knew Father had rescued him from Diego's wrath. Even though neither wanted it this way, there was nothing to do but accept what came next.

It was a short drive, too short for Sam. As they pulled up to the big, stark building that housed the orphanage, it looked more like a manufacturing plant than a home for children.

A fat lady named Carmelo met them at the door. She didn't want Father to go inside, so the adults talked briefly in private before Father and Sam awkwardly said their goodbyes. Sam could tell Father felt terrible about the situation, so he quickly turned and walked into the building as Carmelo held the door. Father yelled that he would visit, but Sam knew it was unlikely given the circumstances. Yet, for a moment, he decided to believe it was true.

I watched as Carmelo waddled ahead of Sam up a dreary staircase. She was wearing an old black dress that rode higher in the back due to her weight. Gripping the handrail, she barked orders between heavy, labored breaths. Sam stopped and looked out the window just in time to see Father's truck turn onto the gravel driveway and disappear up the hill. Carmelo barely noticed he was frozen at the window as she droned on about rules all the way up the stairs. I was crushed to think that Sam might never see my father again.

"Where are you? Move along, boy!" the woman yelled down the staircase, startling Sam as he stood at the window.

Sam followed closely as she showed him the toilet, the bunk beds, and the cafeteria. There was a small locker for him to place his things. Sam knew the cafeteria was where most interactions with the other kids would take place. He looked over the room, filled with benches and tables, and determined which corner he would sit in with his back to the wall. She listed the rules but spent more time emphasizing the punishments for breaking them. She asked Sam questions but never waited for answers. When she was done, she left him sitting on a cot with his rolled-up blanket on his lap, alone.

He looked around to assess the situation, reaching into the blanket to retrieve the little wooden cross. His shoulders sagged as tears rolled down his cheeks.

That day, Sam began planning his escape. It became an obsession. Watching the doors. Noticing when vendors were dropping off supplies. One evening, as a test, he slipped out the main door, walking up the road before returning unnoticed. Once he found the escape route, it became his sole focus.

This morning was his opportunity. There had been a mix-up on an early morning delivery, and an entire row of boxes had toppled over onto a staff member. Sam was in the kitchen when everyone ran to help. He slipped out while the staff was in the storeroom, thinking they would never notice he was gone.

Now he had to accept being caught and that he was in trouble. His foot tapped quickly, relentlessly, on the floor of the car. This nervous tic was new, and it came on when he was anxious or planning something. It was like watching a racehorse waiting for the gate to open. Except there was nowhere to go. No way out. So, he watched and tapped and waited.

The woman in the front seat, his driver, tried to talk to him. "Being in a home is better—and safer—than living on the streets," she said. "Do you want to talk about it?"

Her voice was soft and kind, but Sam refused to engage with her, so she gave up and they rode in silence, with nothing but the sounds of passing traffic and the *tap, tap, tap* of Sammy's foot on the floor.

For Sam, nothing about being caged up in what she called a "home" was better. There was food and a roof, but there was no safety or freedom.

He knew there would be stricter rules and new punishments. At the thought of it all, his heart pounded in his chest. No matter what, he would only endure it for as long as it took him to run again.

8

Flight
Sam

"AWFUL" DIDN'T BEGIN TO describe what it was really like. It was dirty. Disgusting. Full of smells you couldn't identify. They called it an orphanage, but if you saw it, the first word that would come to mind would be "prison." And believe me, that's what it felt like to be locked up in that place. The block walls. The chipping paint on the windowsills. The empty hallways that echoed every sound. It was eerie. Depressing.

For the next two weeks, I stayed strong all day and then cried silently into my pillow when I was in my bunk and the lights were out. Never made a sound. Never even sniffled. It took time, but soon I began to survey the situation. I was figuring out my exit plan, making note of all doors and figuring out which could offer me an easy escape.

My first attempt at running had not gone well. Identified by a neighbor up the street, I was picked up the next morning.

A month later, I had a new plan. I hoarded, stuffing portions of each meal into my pockets. I stole a small pocketknife from one of the boy's lockers. When he realized it was missing, he searched through everyone's beds, lockers, and even other kids' pockets, but never found it. Finding a hiding place for all my treasures was difficult.

At first, I searched in the bathroom for wobbly tiles. I looked in the kitchen during dishwashing duty. Finally, I found a loose baseboard in the stairwell. For a week, I sat down on the stairs, pretending to tie my shoe, and dug a hole in the plaster with a spoon I had taken from the kitchen.

The older boys liked to gamble on the playground. After watching for weeks, I walked over to ask if I could play. The big one pushed me away, making me fall onto the ground. "We don't need any babies in our game," he said, spitting on the ground before turning back to the game.

But I didn't give up. I would stand off to the side and watch their every move. I was younger and smaller, but I was smart. The ringleader was Henry, a big kid with thick wavy hair who wore his shirts too tight. He watched them shoo me away. He noticed me listening and watching.

Henry's body was odd, with short legs but a long, strong torso. He had a scar on his left cheek and a crooked pinky finger on his left hand. One guy had tried to make fun of his name and ended up with a black eye before he finished his joke. One swift smack, his arm jabbing out and in, and it was over.

If there was a calm day, it was because Henry was calm. If there was a fight, Henry was in control of how long the brawl lasted—not always as part of the fight himself but approving the actions with a small nod. The boys were his crew, hanging onto his every word.

One afternoon when they all seemed bored, he told me to come over. "So, you like our games, huh?" he asked, in a voice that seemed too old for a kid.

"Yes, I think I can play," I replied.

He laughed and then looked at his crew, tilting his head. "Okay, go ahead and try."

I should have lost but my competitive nature kicked in and I won the game. I was playing against the boy they called Vato who usually picked on someone and now, was steaming mad at me.

I neglected to consider Vato's ego when I threw the final round of dice and they landed in a pair. The entire crowd went up for grabs, and Vato was on me before I could run. He accused me of cheating, which was ridiculous. How can you cheat the dice? It didn't matter. Soon mob mentality took over and the cheering turned into a fight. Vato wanted to take back my winnings and my confidence, and the boys egged him on.

Henry could have stopped the skirmish, but he simply walked away. He knew there were times when fighting was the only thing to relieve the pressure. There was always pent-up frustration in the orphanage, and it often turned to fistfights. Or he was just trying to teach me a lesson.

I spent the next three days in the infirmary with a broken nose and a fat lip. Someone had stomped on my hand, saying I wouldn't be rolling the dice any time soon. Luckily, none of my fingers were broken.

The quiet time felt good. I was happy being alone. It helped me think and to work on my escape, something that seemed more urgent with every passing day.

The orphanage was designed in wings with a pod for each group of boys. My dorm assignment hitched me to a group of kids who had been street urchins. They grew up fighting for their lives and brought along the dirty tricks they had learned. They didn't worry about violence, they invited it. They didn't think twice about stealing what they needed. These kids were scrappy, and their tolerance for violence was much higher than mine. I knew nothing about surviving on the streets. The fierce competition and intensity of their relationships were new to me.

On one hand, I wanted to gain intelligence for my escape. Those who tried to run away were often caught and returned by either the police or a custodian of the home. The punishments for truancy were handed down swiftly. It wasn't that the orphanage cared so much about the runaway; they didn't like getting in trouble with the authorities.

I knew I wanted—*needed*—a successful escape. I had to leave and avoid being caught. To me, time equaled distance, and the more time that passed before anyone knew I was gone, the farther away I could run. I would get away and be free forever, or so I thought. Boys like me were called "runners," and we were watched like hawks, losing more privileges every time we got into trouble. That meant my plan had to be solid because once I left, I was committed to never coming back.

Beyond the escape itself, I needed to survive once I made it past the fence. What would I eat? Where would I sleep? What dangers would I find on the streets?

Jorge had talked to me about kids he saw along the side of the road on our delivery route. "They are up to no good," he said. He told me to never trust those types of kids. They would do anything to survive, no matter the cost. I wondered if I would become like them, living on the streets, fighting and scraping for survival. No one would trust me. No one would love me.

The beating that sent me to the infirmary made the boys at the orphanage curious. I had not given up any names when interrogated by the staff, and that surprised the older boys. Neither did I answer any questions from the curious kids who surrounded me upon my return. I knew they could easily be stool pigeons and tell the perpetrators. Gaining acceptance from them wasn't worth the risk of another beating.

With my respect level elevated, Henry invited me to hang with the older crowd. It allowed me to learn their quirks and how to "game" the system. I was listening to their stories about the orphanage when one of them talked about an opening in the fence on the back side of the property. Some of the boys used it to leave for short periods, returning through the same hole before being caught.

I asked Max, a boy I'd become friends with, about what I had heard to try to find out the location of the opening. "Have you ever left?" I asked.

"No," he said. "I lived on the streets for a while with my brother, and it was awful. For me, this place is better than that."

"I've heard of guys who leave and come back. Is it true?"

"I've seen it. They go out for the day and others cover for them," he said.

"And no one gets caught?" My curiosity piqued.

"Not often. If they do, the boss lady thinks they're just runners and brings them back."

"Where do they go?" My excitement grew.

"Why do you care?" Max asked. "You can't go anywhere. A little guy like you could never survive on the streets. You have no idea what it's like out there. No family. No home. No money."

I hadn't really considered money. In fact, I didn't know much about money because I hardly ever had any. Jorge dealt with money every day, so I knew what it was. I had collected a few coins over the years, but that was it. The money I did collect was always gone quickly. I would go to the park and ride the little wooden roller-coaster or buy junk food. Most times, I would barter to get what I wanted.

"I don't plan on running, I just want to know," I lied. I never discussed my plan with anyone.

"The boys that run and don't know the path end up walking down the same street every time," Max said. He looked both ways and continued. "The security guards have spies and once informed, they pick them up just blocks from here. The ones who know the secret path have a better chance."

"How do you know there is a path?" I asked, thinking this was just a story Max had made up.

He sat back proudly. "Because I know who leaves and returns."

"What do you mean?"

"They go out and sneak back in the evening," he said. "Some of us know when they go and help cover for them with the caregivers."

"Who goes?"

"I won't tell. You might blab to someone," Max's tone was guarded.

"I won't say anything," I pleaded. I needed information and Max had the whole story.

"No way," he said, shaking his head.

I realized Max would never tell, and in a way, it made me respect him. The boys brave enough to sneak in and out of this place would punish him if he told anyone. I would have to find another way.

"What do they do out there?" I asked, changing the subject.

"I have no idea," he said. "But I don't think it's any better than in here. They always come back."

At that point, I knew Max wasn't the guy to give me the information I was looking for.

Over the next few weeks, I stayed close to the older boys, listening, learning, and gathering any information to help my escape plan. I kept my eye on a boy named Jose. He was a different-looking kid than the rest of us; he had much lighter skin and hair. They sometimes called him *Blanco* (white). He was respected, a quiet guy, second in command behind Henry. The caregivers liked him because he would flash a big smile when they asked the boys to do something. He worked helping the delivery guys, carrying boxes to the clinic. He was better connected than the others.

I noticed there were days when Blanco would be absent and then reappear in the evening. Sometimes he had money. Where did he go? Was he helping? Was he escaping? No one questioned any of this.

One morning in the cafeteria, I sat next to him and tried to strike up a conversation about what went on "on the outside."

"Do you ever go out through the hole in the fence?" I asked. I was hoping to shock him that I knew about the exit and get him to divulge information. Instead, he slowly looked at me, "Where did you hear that?"

Ignoring his question, I continued, "I want to leave, but I don't want to get caught walking down the wrong path or going at the wrong time, you know, when they're watching." As I spoke, I nodded toward the building to indicate the orphanage staff.

"I don't know anything about that," he replied as he stood and walked away.

For the next few weeks, he ignored me, moving away every time I got within a few feet. Henry noticed that I was bothering him.

"What do you want with Blanco?" he asked one day in the yard.

"Nothing," I said.

"Really? Jose doesn't have many friends, so I imagine you are just a pest to him. Be careful, he doesn't like being bothered."

I looked up and realized he wasn't being mean. He was giving me a warning.

I kept my distance from Jose for weeks. Instead, I watched him. He didn't always interact with the boys, but he did like to gamble with them. When they threw dice, he was always there at the center of the game.

My opportunity came one day when Jose decided to play *Dadinho*, a popular dice game. The game consists of each player guessing how many dice showing a certain number, placed under cups, are on the table. The player who loses a round loses one of his dice. The last player to still have dice is the winner.

I had put coins in my shoe for an opportunity just like this. I walked up as they were about to start a new game and put my coins down. I didn't look at anyone. Soon, someone slid a plastic cup with the dice underneath it over to me. The game progressed as I had hoped, with me and Jose as the final two players. It was my turn to throw, and I held the cup in my hand for a second, looking him in the eye without moving.

"If I win, you have to show me," I said in a whisper. He stared back and simply nodded.

When it was over, Jose nodded again and walked away. *I'm in!* I thought.

Each morning, all of us boys woke early to have breakfast in the cafeteria before starting our chores and going to class. Roll call was taken before the food was served. It was always noisy, with rumblings from the tables as we confirmed our presence. It was the same every day; do our chores, then on to class, and afterward, we'd hang out in the courtyard.

The escape came quickly. Jose met me at eight a.m. and told me it was time to go. I had only a moment to run into the stairwell, peel back the woodwork, and stuff the treasures in my pockets. I had collected coins, the pocketknife, food, a bundle of string, and a few bandages.

"What do we tell the teacher?" I asked.

"It's taken care of," he said.

Nothing else was said.

We snuck around the stairwell and out a back door used for deliveries. We stayed close to the side of the building. Once we got to the corner, Jose crossed the driveway to a line of bushes. There was a path next to the fence, and we ducked down as we hurried along. A truck passed, and Jose lay down on the dirt behind a bush. I dove down as well and didn't move until it was out of sight.

We made it through the opening of the fence in no time at all. It was simple. I expected to continue sneaking the whole way, but Jose stood up a short distance from the fence and we walked together across the field like we were strolling down any street. He never looked back. It seemed too easy.

"What's your plan?" he asked as we walked along. I had a feeling of freedom I hadn't felt in a long time, maybe ever.

"I want to leave for good. Make my way out here," I said.

"Maybe you should check it out before you leave for good," he said. "I will tell you when I'm ready to go back, and you can decide what you want to do."

Jose didn't talk the rest of the way. He just stared straight ahead and kept moving.

I walked with my head high and my heart beating out of my chest. Freedom makes you feel like a man. There is no one telling you what to do. No chores. No bells ringing to tell you to eat.

I knew the street would be hard but, at least—and for the first time in my life—I was in control.

9

On the Streets
Jorge

SAM ESCAPED THROUGH AN opening in the fence. Watching him follow Jose gave me a sick feeling. Even in my state, here but not really here, I still felt so many emotions: sadness, hope, anxiety.

I wanted someone to come up from behind, catch them, and take them back to the home. I worried that Jose would abandon Sam, leaving him to fend for himself.

It was obvious Jose knew his way around the village and had a relationship with the street kids in the park. The park was their first stop, and Jose introduced Sam to everyone. They had questions.

"Why are you bringing him here?" said a large boy they called Jefe.

"He wanted to see what it was like on the outside," Jose said. As three more boys gathered, Jose took food out of his pocket and passed it around. I was surprised he was bringing these boys extras from the home. Sam was surprised too.

"What's your story?" another boy, called Red, asked Sam.

Jose answered, "He's okay. He came to the orphanage about six months ago."

"You look like a little punk to me," Red said, ignoring Jose as he walked close to Sam—too close—before circling around him. Red had a scar on his chin, and I wondered if he had fallen or if he'd got it during a fight or a beating.

"He's no punk. He can take it and doesn't squeal," Jose said. Sam appreciated Jose vouching for him.

"I wanted to see what it was like here," Sam said. "I want to leave the orphanage for good."

Another boy, Emilio, who had been eating a piece of the bread Jose brought, spoke next. "You better think twice about that. It might not be easy there, but it's safer than being out here, especially for someone like you." Sam wasn't sure what he meant by that.

A fourth, skinny boy named Loba stared at Sam as he sat atop a nearby picnic table. He seemed jittery and nervous. Suddenly he jumped up, strode over to Sam, and pushed him. "You think you can take it out here?" he asked.

As I expected, Jose didn't interfere. He knew Sam would need to defend himself if he was going to survive outside the orphanage. He crossed his arms and watched the action. Sam took a step back to stop himself from falling but quickly stepped forward. Then, he got right up in Loba's face. "Yes. I can take it," he said, his voice low and determined.

Loba was about to lunge when Jefe grabbed his shoulder. "Leave him alone," he said as he stepped forward and looked Sam up and down. "We can use him. He looks sorta innocent," he said, referring to Sam's small stature and young, unblemished face.

Sam was about to enter a world different from anything he had ever known. I knew he wanted his freedom, but this was not what I wanted for him.

Jefe was obviously in charge. His nickname and size gave it away. The other boys looked to him, but mostly he ignored them, except for Jose. It seemed the two respected each other. How had they formed this friendship? Why did they trust each other?

"Let's get some soda to go with this food," Jefe said, and Jose nodded. The boys started running toward the street and Sam followed.

"We'll teach *el enano* (the runt) how a vending machine works," replied Red over his shoulder.

The boys ran through the park, across the street, and toward a corner where a small bodega supplied food to neighborhood families. Customers, mostly older women, exited in a constant stream, holding bags of groceries tightly as they turned down the street. None of them made eye contact with the boys; they knew better than to engage with street urchins. One woman crossed the street, gripping her bags a little tighter as the group passed.

The store had an entrance from the main street. Surrounding the doors were bins of fruit and vegetables. On the side of the brick building stood an old vending machine next to three garbage cans. A delivery truck was parked in the street. The boys strolled past the building and stood in the lot behind the store. They waited as the driver loaded up a cart to take inside, then when he wheeled it through the door, they approached the vending machine. The truck blocked anyone from seeing what they were up to.

They formed a tight circle. Emilio looked at Sam. "*Enano*, you have the smallest hands. Reach in through the hole and trip the switch. When you pull it down, a can will fall."

Sam stared at him and then at the machine. "What if my arm gets caught in there?"

"Then either the police will find you stuck in there, or we'll cut your arm off," Emilio said, and the boys laughed.

Loba closed in on Sam again—a favorite intimidation tactic of the group. "You're afraid?" he taunted. "That's what I thought."

Sam didn't move.

Jefe looked up and down the street. He was getting impatient. "Do it . . . now," he said. Jefe's command held much more weight and Sam knew it, so he knelt in front of the machine as the guys gathered around him. Reaching into the hole, he felt a switch and he toggled it with his finger. Soon, just like Emilio told him, a can dropped. As if he had something to prove, Sam kept reaching and a second soda dropped.

"A double," Emilio said, grabbing one of the cans from Sam's hand.

Sam handed the other to Jefe, looking him in the eye. "You get the first drink," he said, wanting Jefe to know he respected him.

As I watched, my heart sank. I knew this was the first step in Sam's demise. Stealing was bad, but stealing for fun instead of necessity was worse. It meant he was starting down a new path, away from everything I had taught him. Away from who he was.

After the boys retrieved the soda, they ran back to the park. Under a tree, they pulled out the rest of the food and offered to share it with Jose. He said no. Sam stared at one of the soda cans. Jefe handed it to him, and Sam took a long swig. It was the best drink Sam had ever tasted. Sweet and cold with bubbles that made his nose itch. He smiled genuinely for the first time in months.

The group decided to hang out at the park all day and even played a pickup soccer game with other locals. Late in the afternoon, Jose stood up, caught Sam's attention, and nodded toward the other side of the park. I hoped he would go back with Jose.

"So, what's it gonna be?" Jose asked.

The other boys knew what he meant. They sat quietly, watching and waiting.

Sam wanted out of the home, but the day had given him a dose of reality about the outside world. He was conflicted.

Jose looked at him for a moment and then said, "Let's go back. You can always come again."

Jefe walked over to Sam, getting uncomfortably close. "Do what he says," Jefe whispered.

Sam followed but looked over his shoulder at the four guys sitting under the tree. He had a million questions. He wondered if they would have accepted him had he stayed. They didn't seem to care either way. He wanted his freedom but, in the moment, didn't have the confidence. I was relieved.

Jose didn't say a word as they made the long walk back. Sam didn't either. This day had proven to Sam that freedom came with a price.

The boys quietly slipped back through the orphanage's fence, crawled along the bushes, and walked into the building through the back entrance. They'd missed dinner but no one was looking for them. Sam was relieved.

In their bunk room, one of the kids approached Sam. "What's it like out there? Great?" he asked smiling.

Sam looked up at him. "Out where?" he said. "I was here all day." Jose smirked and nodded his approval.

That night, Sam lay awake for a long time, tossing, turning, and thinking about what could have been and what might still be. When he did finally fall asleep, it was restless and fitful.

The next day, and for a time after, Sam seemed happier. The power of knowing he could leave was enough to help him endure. And, as rumors circulated about the recent trip to town, he earned a new level of respect from the older boys at the orphanage.

One particularly sweltering day, Sam was in the courtyard when the older boys decided to play soccer. He was fast, so he was one of the first players chosen. The game was going well, and Sam had no trouble keeping up with the older boys. Early on, Sam received a pass and drove the ball toward the goal. He swung his leg for a shot but missed the ball, and instead, connected solidly with Vato's ankle. For a moment, Vato writhed in pain, but then jumped up and went after Sam. Henry was across the field and too far away to intervene.

"Take it easy, Vato!" Henry yelled as he ran toward them, but Vato was already landing blows to the side of Sam's head. Sam's arms were up around his ears to protect himself from the punches.

Vato looked at Henry without letting go of Sam's shirt. "Who are you to tell me what to do?" he asked disdainfully.

Everyone froze, including Vato. I knew what would come next. Everyone did. Henry was the leader, and if he wanted to keep his place, he would have to defend himself.

He walked slowly toward Vato, who tossed Sam aside.

"I don't know why we all listen to you," Vato said to Henry. "Maybe it's time to see just how tough you are."

The two boys lunged at each other while the others backed away. Both threw punches, and soon it was easy to see this would be an even match. Henry's nose was covered in blood and Vato's lip was sliced open. The two fell to the ground and started rolling around. Henry was stronger, but Vato was fierce and fast with his return punches. He could move quickly and easily, making Henry, who was big but slow, miss.

For a few minutes, Jose stood and watched. Eventually, he hit the arm of a boy next to him, and they moved into the middle of the fight. Vato was no match once the others engaged.

When it was over, Carmelo and the cook announced a lockdown. Henry and Vato went to the clinic, and everyone else was confined to their beds for the night.

The two boys showed up the next day covered in bruises and bandages.

The environment in the dorm changed then. Everyone became more guarded and chose their words carefully. In the courtyard, Vato stood at one end and Henry at the other. Sam stood with Henry, which made me happy. Vato was a punk. Granted, they were all punks, but Vato had no conscience and only thought of himself.

A few days later, Vato was lying on his bed and Henry was at his locker when the dorm door swung open. Carmelo led two police officers into the room. "I just don't understand how you think Henry could be the one to steal from the church," she said.

"The information we received matches his description and we were told he lives here," the sergeant said.

"Henry, these men want to talk with you," Carmelo said.

"Me? Why?" he asked as he turned to face her and the officers.

"They say you snuck out of here and stole a chalice from the sacristy at the church," she said.

"I'll do the questioning," the sergeant interrupted.

"I was never at the church—" Henry began.

The sergeant pushed him aside and began rifling through Henry's locker. Clothes spilled out onto the floor. Then the sergeant grabbed a black cloth from under a pair of pants. He unwrapped it to reveal a beautiful gold chalice.

"I don't know how that got there!" Henry yelled.

"Let's talk about that at the police station," the sergeant said, nodding to his partner, who grabbed Henry by the arm as he continued to argue his innocence.

"I don't know how he could have done that," Carmelo said, following them out. "We take diligent care of these boys. They have no reason to steal."

Henry looked back and his eyes met Vato's. Vato waved and blew him a kiss. It had been a setup. How had Vato put the chalice in Henry's locker? How had he alerted the authorities? No one knew, but Henry was later charged with stealing, and we were told he ended up in the boy's detention center.

For the next few weeks, the whole place was on edge. Sam stayed away from everyone, knowing he had instigated the incident on the soccer field.

One of Sam's chores was to sweep the dorm floors with an old broom. He moved the lockers to clean behind them and he found a little cross on the floor near Henry's bed. He had seen Henry wearing it and realized it must have fallen when the police searched his locker. Sam looked around and quickly stuffed the cross into his pocket.

Later that afternoon, Sam was sitting in the stairwell pretending to tie his shoe. Once he was alone, he removed the secret panel from the wall of his hiding space. He pulled the cross from his pocket and was about to wrap it in a cloth when a hand grabbed his shoulder.

It was Vato.

"What is this?" he asked.

Before Sam could hide his belongings, Vato grabbed the cloth. He jumped down to the landing and opened it. In his hand laid coins, the cross, the pocketknife, and a few small trinkets.

"So, you're a thief," he said.

"No, I found those things," Sam said, reaching for the cloth.

Vato pushed him back. "Let's see what the guys think about your treasures."

He ran down the stairs and Sam followed him to the courtyard.

"Hey guys, look at this!" Vato yelled as he approached the group, assembled along the fence line. "Sam has been stealing from everyone, even poor Henry."

The boys gathered around to look at what Vato had in his hands.

"That's Henry's cross," someone said.

Another boy chimed in, "And that keychain is mine."

Jose pushed forward and grabbed Sam. "That's my pocketknife."

"Let me explain," Sam said, desperately trying to produce a story as he stood before this jury of his peers, people Sam didn't even know when he took most of these things.

"You stole from me . . . from me!" Jose was incredulous and furious.

Before Sam could respond, Jose hit him in the face, grabbed the knife, and walked away. The blow landed squarely on Sam's nose, and by the time staff arrived to see what had happened, blood was gushing from both nostrils as well as a cut on the bridge of his nose.

In the infirmary, Sam was questioned about the fight. Who hit you? How did this start? He never revealed a thing. He just lay quietly in the bed near the nurse's station, wishing he could talk to Jose. Even if he could explain, there was no good excuse for what he had done.

10

Working the Streets
Sam

I COULD NOT STAY. I had to get away from this place; a place where I was completely singled out and ostracized.

I was in the infirmary for the night; safe from any further beatings with time to figure out my next move. This time, there would be no plan to return, so there was no need to worry about morning roll call. Once the nurse was out of sight tending to another kid, I would simply slip out the back door.

Soon, the opportunity presented itself. I remembered the path: behind the bushes, down the road, and out through the opening in the chain link fence. I walked across the field, but this time I didn't feel empowered. I looked back, wondering if I was being followed. This was not freedom, it was an escape. Survival. Going back would be unbearable. Moving forward might be unbearable too, but I had no choice.

I walked to the park, looking for Jefe. He was under a tree with Emilio and Loba, and they recognized me right away.

"Sam, what happened to you?"

I had forgotten about my face, the pain dulled by my obsession to escape. I walked up and sat down, deciding to tell them everything. I told them the story about Vato and Henry, but I left out the fact that it was Jose's pocketknife I had stolen.

Jefe listened, taking it in and trying to figure out what it all meant, for me and for him.

"I was hoping I could hang with you guys," I said.

Emilio was the first to answer. "Well, you can replace Red," he said. "He got himself arrested for stealing from the bodega. How stupid could he be, getting caught stealing an orange and in his pocket no less?" He was laughing, and soon, the other boys were too. All except Jefe.

Loba was staring at me. He was not going to help me so I kept looking at Jefe.

"We have a job that starts tomorrow, and they said I could bring as many guys as I wanted," Jefe said. "So, if you want to stay and work, that's fine."

Loba turned his head quickly to Jefe who spoke without giving him a chance to contest the decision. "He can help us as a decoy," Jefe said, not offering any details.

I had managed to pocket some food before I escaped the infirmary and pulled it out of my pocket. I wasn't going to share if they dumped me, but now, it was a peace offering.

We ate as the sun went down. The boys each ripped off pieces of the bean *papusas*. I knew the feeling of hunger, but it was nothing like what they experienced. Their need for food was primal.

As darkness came, the guys told me to follow them. I assumed they slept in the park, but Emilio explained they would be in trouble with the police if they were caught out after curfew.

As we walked down a dirt road along the river, Jefe talked about the upcoming job. We would work on fruit trucks, unloading produce at each stop. The fruit was in season, which meant they had to move it quickly. That's where we came in—as seasonal help.

"The pay isn't good, but we'll get a few coins, plus they'll feed us," Jefe explained. "And we'll get to taste the best watermelon, oranges, and bananas in the world."

We came upon a bridge, and the boys ducked under the side. This was where the boys holed up at night. Under the bridge's concrete pylons, they had each staked out a spot using towels and rags rolled up near little piles of clothes and trinkets. Each cubby was "home" to one of the boys.

"You can take Red's spot over there," Jefe said, pointing between the bridge's diagonal beams as he laid out an old blanket for himself.

I watched each of them prepare for the night and noticed a few treasures tucked in the corner of Red's space: a small stuffed animal, a plastic cup, and an old jacket. I assumed this was what he slept on.

"Where is Red now?" I asked.

"Probably in boy's detention," Jefe said. "The authorities don't take lightly to thieves who steal from the bodegas."

No one else spoke after that. After rearranging Red's things, I lay there thinking about the detention center and what it would be like. Was it worse than the orphanage?

I awoke stiff, and it took a moment to remember where I was—sleeping on concrete under a bridge. It was summer but the damp, dark place made me shiver. The other boys were still sleeping. I decided to lay still and not do anything until someone else woke. This place was like nothing I had ever experienced. I knew I should fear what might happen or be disgusted with sleeping under a bridge, but I felt liberated. Strong. And safer than I had since Jorge died.

Soon the boys were awake. By noon, we had to meet the man who would hire us for the deliveries. We walked to a loading area where trucks were backing in, and men yelled out orders to one another. The group waited outside the gate while Jefe went to talk with the boss. He reappeared with a fat man in dirty jeans and a black T-shirt who looked each of us up and down as if we had just joined the military. When he finished his inspection, he simply walked away and waved for us to follow.

We were told to get inside the trucks in pairs. At each stop, the driver would tell us how much to unload, and we would move large boxes of fruit from the truck to the store or fruit stand.

I was paired up with Emilio, who took the spare tire as his seat in the back of the truck. I sat on a crate and soon learned I had to jam it into the corner so it didn't slide around when the truck was moving. The boss told us we could eat only the fruit given to us by our driver, but of course, the moment the door closed, we each grabbed a banana and shoved it in our mouths. It was the best-tasting banana of my life.

My nerves were tingling. I wasn't sure I felt good, but I certainly felt free. We slept along the road each night. Our driver gave us a blanket to spread out on the ground. He slept in the cab of the truck with the doors locked.

Emilio and I stared up at the dark sky.

"Before she died, my mother loved to look at the stars," he said. "She had names for them and said they made shapes of things, like animals and gods."

"How did she die?"

"My father was never around. She had a boyfriend, and they were both shot walking down the street one night. He was part of a gang," he said it like it didn't matter, like it was ancient history. "I was little."

"Did you see it happen?" I asked.

"No. The police came to our door and took me and my sister," he replied, reaching into his back pocket. "I keep this photo of her."

It was too dark outside to see it well, but I stared at it for a long time anyway.

"I never knew my mother," I said. "She threw me in the trash when I was a baby."

"That's harsh," he said, still with little emotion. "At least I have my memories."

"Yeah, but I don't feel any pain about her."

After that we were quiet.

The next morning, we were back on the job, driving from stop to stop, unloading the truck. To pass the time, we played games or made up crazy stories about people we met at the stands or in the shops.

"The old man with the walking stick was kicked out by his wife," I said when it was my turn to start a story. "He's been on that chair outside the store for three months waiting for her to come and get him."

"Yeah, well the little girl in the store is his grandchild, and he sits there to protect her from *banditos*," Emilio said.

For four days, we rode in the truck. We made stops at grocery stores, gas stations, and roadside markets. Finally, the truck was empty, and we lay down on the cold metal floor for the drive back. When we arrived, our driver opened the tailgate to reveal the fat man, the big boss, standing at the bumper.

"Come back tomorrow morning," he said. "You can help deliver a load of watermelons." Then he spit on the ground and walked away.

I was excited to eat watermelon. I had never tasted it, and the other boys said it was sweet like candy. We returned in the morning and climbed into the back of the truck. This time, there was almost no place to sit because the melons were so large. I climbed along the side and nestled between the melons in the pile as the truck started moving.

The weather was extremely hot and the melons were very heavy. After three days of hefting each watermelon off the truck, we were exhausted. Fortunately, Emilio and I had watermelon to eat, and it was delicious. We would drop a melon from over our heads and let it crack in half. If it broke into two pieces, we would each take one and start chomping on the delicious red center. My whole body felt sticky from the juice residue on my face, arms, and legs.

When we got back "home," we were dirty and tired. We walked toward our spots under the bridge in silence. We had been working for days.

Jefe and Loba had already returned. When we sat down, Jefe pulled out a bar of soap. "Anyone interested in getting clean?"

"Where did you get that?" Emilio asked.

I didn't care. I was delighted and just wanted to wash up. Besides regular meals, showering was the thing I missed most from my old life. I loved feeling the water flowing over my body and then drying off with a towel, even the thin, rough towels at the orphanage.

Jefe took the soap and headed for the river. We jumped in fully clothed and started splashing and laughing. The water was high from recent heavy rains in El Salvador. As it ran down from the mountains, the river widened and the current moved faster.

I took off my pants and shirt and scrubbed them with soap. After washing, rinsing, and wringing out each piece of clothing, I held them above my head, walking toward shore. I made my way against the current to a little tree and hung my shirt and pants to dry. Now it was time to use the soap on my body. It was hard and not at all fragrant, but it felt like an entire layer of dirt fell off my skin.

Emilio wanted the soap, and I carefully walked the bar over to him, holding it high. If I dropped it in the river, it would be gone for good.

After my bath, I decided to lie down for some well-deserved sleep. Red's spot had become my place, and it felt like home. The bridge protected us from the weather but also offered a hiding spot; a safe zone that limited the ways anyone could come after us.

Under the bridge, there was a long concrete block with diagonal beams every four feet or so. The beams provided little nooks for each of us. Just like anyone's home, I set up my spot with things I'd collected. The banana trip allowed me to pick up three new trinkets, and I lined them up neatly. I had found a U.S. penny, a hair clip, and a pencil. I don't know why I kept the pencil since we had no paper, but when you have nothing, anything is a treasure.

I remember lying on my back listening to the guys talking in the river. Soon, I was asleep.

The worst part of our living situation was the mosquitos. They swarmed around the riverbank, and with no breeze to keep them at bay, we had bites from head to toe.

When I awoke, rain was falling and I was shivering. I realized I had gone to sleep with only shorts on and my clothes were still hanging on the tree. Crawling to the edge of the bridge cover, I could see the river had risen even higher overnight. To my right, the little tree I'd hung my clothes on was partially underwater and only four articles of clothing clung to the branches. My pants were fully submerged in the river but holding onto a branch by a belt loop.

"Guys, get up. Our clothes are gone!" I yelled. I hurried toward the tree, grabbing my pants and the three other items as the guys started peeking out from the bridge underpass.

My shirt was gone. Emilio's too. It meant we would have to find a clothesline and "shop" for something new. The stealing didn't seem like a terrible thing anymore. We only took what we really needed. Necessity—not greed—was our motivator, and that seemed better than just taking things for no reason, or worse yet, for fun. We were either naked or hungry and always desperate for something.

Once our food truck job finished and we had spent our wages, we went back to being hungry all the time. Loba had an idea to get money for food. We were spending our days around the street market, and he had noticed a lady who ran a small restaurant. Every Tuesday, she would buy groceries for the restaurant. At the register, Loba had seen her pull out a bag filled with cash. Since then, he had hung around to watch her when she went to the market. He knew her exact route from the restaurant to the market and back home. His plan was to steal her bag, as she never spent all the money and would have her hands full of groceries on the walk back.

Loba pointed out the woman and we followed her. I was to distract her by approaching her and asking a question. "If you beg, she will probably stop to give you a piece of fruit," he said. "When she's distracted, we'll grab the cash."

From afar, she didn't look like anyone I should care about, just a stranger carrying bags down the street. The path back to her restaurant took her past a quiet street that was perfect for our plan.

I was waiting at the end of the block. As soon as she turned the corner, I started to walk toward her to stop her near the alley by an old house. Jefe was waiting there. We decided he was the biggest and fastest in the group. Emilio and Loba would follow.

As she approached, she looked different from how I thought she would. She had a kind face, and her hair, pulled back into a bun, reminded me of Jorge's wife, Rosa. There were laugh lines on her face along the sides of her lips and at the corner of her eyes. She didn't have the deep frown lines on her brow like many other women did. She walked with deliberation and looked into my eyes. I was hoping I wouldn't give away my intent.

"Hola," I said. "Do you have any food or money to spare?"

She peered at me with no emotion, looking up and down the street before deciding whether I was worthy of help. I stayed back just as Loba instructed, giving her space and gaining her trust. She set down her groceries and reached in her purse to give me something. At that instant, Jefe jumped out, grabbed her purse, reached in for the bag of money, and threw the purse on the ground.

"RUN!" he yelled.

I remember the woman staring me straight in the eye. It seemed like time stood still. I felt her deep disappointment and anger. She didn't even try to chase Jefe. There was an instant sense of defeat, both mine and hers. She turned to yell at Jefe as I turned and ran in the other direction. I never looked back. I didn't need to—her face would be etched in my brain forever.

The guys were already back under the bridge, planning what to do with the money when I got there.

"That was impressive," Jefe exclaimed as he sat in his nook, counting the cash.

"For the next few weeks, the two of us will have to stay here," Jefe explained. "Loba and Emilio will go buy the food. Things will have to die down with the cops; that is, if she even called them."

That night, I couldn't sleep. I was restless, and every time I closed my eyes all I could see was her face. The disappointment. The disgust. I knew she worked hard for her money, and the loss would be devastating to her family. Yet, I tried to rationalize our decision. What else could we do? We needed to survive. We were desperate.

Jorge popped into my thoughts. He always talked about a "man's soul" and how honesty and hard work built a lifetime of honor. I would be a disappointment to him now. In his eyes, there was nothing to justify my actions. But Jorge wasn't here. I was on my own.

We had food for quite a while. Loba bought chicken, rice, and beans. This was special because, for once, the food was hot. We ate it under the bridge. Those were the most delicious meals of my life.

After weeks in hiding, I was getting restless. Emilio and Loba were free to move around, but Jefe and I stayed either in the park or under the bridge.

"When can we go back to the market?" I asked.

"You need to wait at least a month," Jefe explained. "If we see the woman or police looking for you, it will be longer."

The money lasted a long time. We had food for more than two weeks. I was learning the importance of cash and how good it felt to have it.

The next few months passed quickly. The rainy season was coming up, and the guys warned that we might have to move if the rains became too heavy and the river rose to flood under the bridge.

Eventually, Jefe and I went back into town and to the market. I wasn't nervous, but it was obvious Jefe was looking over his shoulder more than ever.

Emilio and Loba had a plan to steal cash from a street vendor. A man who sometimes left his adult son in charge of their station had tables loaded with electronics. There were batteries, mini radios, CD players, watches, and even phones. Nothing was in its packaging, so we assumed the products were either fake or stolen. The spaces were tight, and the man watched everything like a hawk. He had set up mirrors on either end of his stall so he could watch his merchandise from any vantage point. His son was not as attentive, and the guys figured he would be an easy target. Jefe explained that each of us would stand in a different spot. Then we would make movements or noises to distract the son while Jefe grabbed the cash from the drawer. I stood on a corner near the phone cases, pretending I was looking for something and ignoring the son like Jefe had instructed. I kept looking up and, from the corner of my eye, I saw the son's eyes dart back and forth between all of us.

Emilio was the first to drop something. As he did, the son jumped off his chair. Then I picked up a case and dropped it, except mine hit the table instead of the ground. The son ran over to Emilio. "What are you doing? Get away from here!" he yelled.

By the time he moved back to his chair, Jefe was already walking away, and we took off to follow him. We didn't get far. The father and two police officers surrounded us. The bigger police officer put a hand on Jefe. "Let me see what you have in your pocket," he said.

Jefe held out his empty hand, "What?" he asked, but his innocent face was no match for this guy.

"Come with me," he said.

They had been ready for us. The man and the police were watching the market the whole time. They had seen Jefe take the money. They had seen all of us take part. The scammers had been scammed.

As we walked to the police van, we saw the woman we had robbed weeks before. She stood with her arms crossed, glaring at me, waiting for her revenge.

"Is this the boy who stole your money?" the police officer asked her.

"Yes," she said. I could hear the anger and the disappointment in her voice.

"And the others? Were they with him?"

She looked into my eyes, and I looked at my feet. I couldn't meet her gaze. I was too ashamed. Then, her tone softened. "What happens to them?" she asked sympathetically.

"The older ones will go to juvenile detention," the police officer said.

"Maybe, I am not sure about this one," she said, pointing at me. I knew she was covering for me but I didn't know why.

The police didn't care. As we sat in the van, Jefe and the others said nothing. I had no idea what would happen next, but their body language told me it was bleak.

II

I'm Home

Sam

I NEVER SAW JEFE or the other boys again. I was too young for the detention center, so they separated me from them at the police station. I was told to wait in a chair, and a social worker appeared at the desk, filed papers, and walked me out the door.

I stared out the window the entire ride back to the orphanage, plotting my next escape. My knee bounced up and own. I was nervous; a caged animal ready to run again the first chance I had. If running away was as simple as opening the car door, I would have done it. But I had nowhere to go. My friends were no longer under the bridge and the police would find me.

I wondered who would find our stuff. Would other kids occupy our beds and adopt our trinkets?

I dreaded going back to the orphanage. Jose had never visited the entire time I was on the streets. Did he know I would be there? Was he trying to avoid me? If he had visited, I would have explained the pocketknife and asked him to forgive me.

Everything about the orphanage was running through my head. I hated the smell. I hated the bell ringing to tell me when to eat. Would Jose be angry? Was Henry back? Would Vato pick up where he left off?

People think being on the street is no place for a kid, but it was so much better than going back to the orphanage. On the outside, I controlled my destiny. I had no calendar to mark the time but guessed it was close to a year since I had run away. I survived with my friends. We'd created a home of our own. We were equals with common goals. Find work. Eat. Hang out. Survive.

Once I was caught, the social workers decided sending me back to the orphanage was the best choice. Did they have any idea how bad it was? Had they ever visited or even talked to anyone at this awful place? I understood why they were sending me back; there was nowhere else for me to go, no one in my life. I hated them all: the police, the social workers, and the caregivers. And as I walked through the orphanage door, my anger grew.

Back to the same dorm room. A new kid was in my old bunk, but I didn't care. The boys eyed me up. Vato came over to tell me he'd be watching. The rest gave me the cold shoulder. Jose was nowhere to be found.

Since I was considered a "runner," the caregivers took away all my privileges. Besides chores and class, there was little else for me. No time in the courtyard. No recreation. And I was forced to regularly check in with the staff. I spent the next month speaking to no one. I had a routine. Wake up. Roll call. Chores. Eat. School. Bed.

I knew eventually I would escape again. But I told no one and gave no indication of any kind. Soon the weeks turned to months and the months turned to years.

One evening, Carmelo came to the dorm and called out twelve names, including mine. We were told to go to the cafeteria. After we sat in rows on the benches, she explained that there was a new orphanage opening and we were being moved. I was part of a group of boys selected to live there. No one told us why or asked if we wanted to go. As much as I hated where I was, the last thing I wanted was to start over again, reliving the same horrors.

I felt powerless, hopeless, and was convinced the new place would be another version of this one. We were told to pack our things, get a good night's sleep, and meet in the yard first thing in the morning for instructions.

"Bring everything," they said, "because you're not coming back."

The next morning as the bus pulled up, all I could think of was that my tragic life was changing again, not for the better, just a different version of this. It was déjà vu in the worst conceivable way.

In the main courtyard, tired, confused, and hungry, we were given a small sack of food for the trip. Minutes later, I would be on a small bus being taken from one hell hole only to be dropped into another. I looked down at the transfer paper they had handed me. It said "2002." It was the first time in years I thought about time or dates. It meant I was 13 years old.

I remembered that Jorge always knew the date and loved June first. He said it marked the end of the rainy season and the start of summer.

I took a seat in the back of the bus, like always, to keep everyone where I could see them and be aware of any trouble that might start. We were told nothing about this new place, and even though I hated where I had been living, at least it was familiar. The disgusting food, the bullying, and the occasional abuse by staff. I knew how to navigate things, but more importantly, I knew the route for my escape.

The motor roared and the bus lurched forward as it turned left out of the driveway of the home, taking me to the next phase of my life. I could hardly stomach the anxiety. *How will I escape this new place? Where will I go when I run? What's around the corner?* I was back to square one.

As the trip progressed, my life played out before my eyes. With every mile, I was reminded of where I had been. I thought about my mother and father, people I never knew, and fantasized about how life might have been different if they hadn't abandoned me.

I remembered Jorge, his stoic face, absent of emotion, always wondering if he loved me, but never doubting that he cared. I recalled the wonderful smell of his bread truck and helping him make deliveries.

And the shooting. Oh, my God, it seemed like a lifetime ago, yet the fear, the hatred for the men who robbed us, and the deep sadness were as fresh as when it happened. I rubbed the back of my head, tracing the scar the bullet had left behind. My nerves still tingled when I touched it. The sensation comforted me; a reminder that Jorge was still with me, a part of my life.

Passing through a village, I saw a man shouting at a young boy and pulling him by the arm. It made me think of Diego, the man who I had hoped would save me and give me a new life after Jorge died. Unfortunately, Diego didn't see me as the son or the nephew he never had. I was just an indentured servant to him, property he used and abused for his own gain and pleasure. Alonzo had tried to save me from the abuse.

I remembered him saying, "Samuelito, I pray for you to be gone from this house." His prayer had been answered, but it landed me at the orphanage and then on the streets. It had proven to be so much worse than living with Diego.

What I wouldn't give to be back there again, lying safely in my closet.

An hour passed, and I sat silently and gazed out the window at everything and nothing at all. All of us sat quietly. There was nothing to talk about. The boys were from different dorms. We didn't know each other. At times, my focus was clear and my senses on high alert. Other times, I'd check out as the miles clicked off, the sun moving from east to west.

I noticed traffic increasing around the bus and sat up, wondering if we were getting close to our destination. Then I saw a sign on the road. Santa Ana. Could we be back near Diego's house? I tried to remember the streets and wondered if given the chance, could I make my way back there? *Maybe if I found Alonzo, he would take me in. Was he alive? Maybe if I talked to Diego about working harder, he would take me back. I'm older and stronger. He'd see me as more of a partner, someone who can really help him.*

We passed through the town and I sat up tall, looking for familiar things. *Was that the store I used to walk through, looking at all the items but without money to buy anything? Is that the street we walked down?* It all looked familiar, but at the same time, I couldn't place anything. I looked back as the town disappeared, hoping to recognize something, anything. Even Diego.

Once we were out of town, I sat looking forward. *Was it really that bad at Diego's house?* I started to imagine it wasn't. Eventually, I closed my eyes and dozed off.

As the bus turned, the sunlight hit my face and a terrible smell woke me. I knew that smell even before I opened my eyes.

It was a garbage dump, but in El Salvador, it was also home to people who couldn't find a better option. Poverty was everywhere, forcing people to rummage through garbage dumps for food and shelter. Jorge found me in a garbage dump just like this one. It was massive, trash as high and as far as the eye could see. But it's not the garbage that draws one's attention. It's the people going through the dump for food and treasure; from the youngest children (some of whom were born here) to parents and old people.

I was numb to it all. Today was just another page of an awful book.

I was hungry. The lunch we were given to eat on the bus was long gone, my stomach was growling, and I was hot. It's always hot here, but the prolonged heat was affecting me more than usual. The others, some who'd become nervously talkative and annoying, had quieted down as the hours passed. Some slept. Others, like me, simply stared out the window, watching the scenery change and wondering how our collective lives would change in the coming days, months, and years.

I was half sitting, half lying on the seat, hoping to fall back asleep. This time, it wasn't the smell that jolted me, it was the bumpy dirt road and the grinding of brakes. I looked out to see we were as the bus approached a large gate with a high brick wall topped with barbed wire. Above the gate was a sign, *Nuestros Pequeños Hermanos* (Our Little Brothers & Sisters).

We had arrived, but all I could think was *These people aren't my brothers.*

At first, it looked like a jail, but as the gate opened slowly, it revealed a beautiful, tree-lined courtyard with a paved circle drive leading up to a big building.

Now we were all awake, sitting upright and alert, foreheads against the windows, our eyes wide. No one said a word, we just took in the new surroundings. Slowly, the bus pulled through the gate and up the path. This was not like the place I had left hours ago, at least not from the outside.

Smiling children ran and played in the courtyard, waving to us, *los nuevos hermanos.* The bus stopped and the children gathered around. They seemed eager to meet us. The bus door swung open, and we slowly emerged into the late afternoon heat. A group of children parted, and an adult, a *padre*, approached. He was a clean and well-groomed *gringo* wearing shorts and sandals. The only thing distinguishing him as a priest was his black shirt and white collar. Otherwise, just another white man. I had seen them before.

I'd find out later his name was Father Ron. But at that moment, I wasn't sure what to make of him, this place, or what was going to happen. A scene that looked too good to be true to a boy who didn't even know what "too good to be true" meant. I remember looking back at the gate, devising a way out.

My plan? To run at the first chance.

I2

NPH
Jorge

I WATCHED AS SAM navigated this strange place. He was confused and so was I. The happiness seemed almost surreal.

Sam went with the other boys to the medical clinic where a nurse checked him out. She was young and friendly, asking him questions he didn't answer, but she didn't seem to care. Next, he was taken across the courtyard to the school where he met his new teacher, another young woman with a bright smile. After that, a boy named Mario walked the group of boys around the whole campus, naming each building and explaining daily routines. Not one of the new boys spoke.

Mario escorted each boy to their respective dorm room, showing them the bathrooms and the lockers where they were to neatly fold and put away their things. Sam sat down on his assigned bed. Another boy from the bus who was also assigned to the room tried to strike up a conversation with Sam, but he paid no attention.

After unpacking the few items he carried with him, Sam headed for the dining hall. As he stepped through the door, he stopped in his tracks. Through the doorway to the kitchen, he saw a familiar face. Jose was cleaning dishes at a huge sink and laughing with two other boys. He must have been transferred to NPH while Sam was on the streets. It explained why he was gone when Sam was captured and returned, and maybe why he never visited the boys again while Sam was on the streets.

Sliding behind another boy, Sam ducked out the door and returned to his dorm. I knew he didn't know what to do next. How would Jose treat him after the pocketknife incident? What could Sam say to make him understand?

Sam didn't have much time to think. A group of boys entered the room and Jose walked in with them. As he passed, Jose noticed Sam. He stopped to stare. Sam knew it was all coming back. Then he walked to his bunk without saying a word.

When Sam woke the next morning, Jose was gone. He followed a group of boys to the dining hall, looking over his shoulder the whole way. I knew that feeling; waiting for something bad to happen but not knowing when it would come. He was on edge, expecting the other shoe to drop. Like a robot, he went from the dining hall to the school to the playground, scanning for Jose the entire time.

Throughout the day, Sam followed the assigned schedule, from the dorm to the medical office to receive vaccinations, to class, and finally, to the cafeteria again for dinner. I couldn't believe how smoothly things ran at this place. Children were talking and laughing, walking their trays back to long tables from the food line. Sam placed himself behind a small boy, leaning forward to see what was for dinner. He was starving.

There, standing behind the huge bin of beans with a large metal spoon in his hand, was Jose. Sam put down his tray and went outside. I assumed he wanted to avoid confrontation in the dining hall. I thought he might have the courage to talk to Jose, but instead, he returned to his dorm early and pretended to be asleep.

The next morning, Sam woke before anyone else and went over to the cafeteria building, waiting for Jose under a tree. This time, he saw him strolling across the lawn and Sam stepped out.

"Jose," he said.

Walking over to Sam, he placed his hands on his hips. "So, we meet again. How was your time on the streets?"

"I want to explain the pocketknife," Sam started. "I never meant to steal from you. I had taken it much earlier from a random locker, long before I knew it was yours."

"So that makes it okay?" Jose asked sarcastically.

"No, I wanted you to know it was never directed at you," Sam said, trying to appear calm and confident.

"You shouldn't steal from anyone," Jose said.

"I know."

"This place isn't like the others. The kids here are kind and trust each other. Don't bring your bad habits here." Then, Jose left. It surprised us both. No violence. No argument. I decided I liked him.

Sam wasn't sure what to do. He had never known anyone quite like Jose, but he didn't have time to think about it as the day's routine continued. Sam went through the schedule, doing what he was told without much emotion or thought.

"How are you, Sam? This is day three, right?" a voice said behind him in the lunch line.

Sam turned around, startled at hearing his name. It was the *padre* who had greeted the bus on the first day. He was a young man with a happy, sincere face. Today, he wore shorts and sandals, but with a T-shirt instead of the clerical collar. He was thin and moved quickly as the kids constantly surrounded him, the little ones pulling on his shirt to get his attention and tell him a story. I liked him, too. But Sam? Not so much. He was suspicious.

Sam looked up at the priest's smiling face. "How are you finding it here?" asked the priest.

"Okay," Sam said nervously. He had never really spoken to a priest.

"Sam, I get to know all the kids here," Father Ron said. "I would like you to meet with me for a short talk each week. How about Monday mornings? Be in my office at nine a.m."

It was obvious this meeting was not up for discussion. He turned to talk to two small boys and went on his way. Sam stared at his back.

The first Monday shortly before nine, Sam walked to the office building on the grounds and found Father Ron's office. The building had concrete floors and brightly painted hallways. At the office door, he peered around the corner.

"Come in, Sam," Father Ron said.

Father Ron introduced himself and talked almost nonstop. He told Sam about himself: He was from the United States, somewhere near Chicago. He had volunteered as a young man with Father Wasson, the priest who started the NPH orphanages in Mexico. There, he was called to serve God and decided to become a priest.

As I listened, I could feel the deep love Father Ron had for NPH. He told stories of all the kids he had known, both in Mexico and now, in Central America. Father Ron was the director of the four Central American homes and was assigned to live in El Salvador for five years.

I was amazed at his story and his fluent Spanish. He felt like someone who belonged here, yet he looked nothing like anyone I had ever seen.

Sam sat in the chair in front of his desk, listening and fidgeting with his fingers, something he did when he was uncomfortable. When Father Ron told him he could leave, Sam almost jumped out of the chair.

Sam went to Father Ron's office every week for a month. The next meetings were different. Father Ron would ask Sam a question and then sit quietly, waiting to draw him out. He was relaxed, and the quiet tension made Sam nervous. The interactions were awkward, yet the priest knew so much could be said with silence.

I liked Father Ron and wished Sam would open up. He was patient, asking questions but often receiving one-word answers. I wanted him to experience Sam's happy side and the way his face lit up a room when he smiled. I also wanted Father Ron to see Sam's true personality; his "fun" side. I remembered a day when Sam was trying to teach my girls how to juggle. He was proud of his skill, and they were all laughing as he patiently explained how to catch rolled-up socks thrown from one hand to another.

That was the Sam I wanted everyone to know. But, after all the things that had happened, I was worried that fun Sam didn't exist anymore. Was he still in there?

At the end of their next meeting, Father Ron had his hand on the office doorknob, about to end the session, when Sam blurted out, "I don't like it here."

"Why, Sam?" he asked, taking his hand off the doorknob and facing Sam.

"I don't like the boys."

"Anyone in particular giving you trouble?"

Sam looked up at him. "All of them, even *el niño sin piernas* (the kid with no legs)."

"You mean Juan Manuel?" Father Ron asked, knowing exactly who Sam was talking about.

"He's an ass," Sam said under his breath. He knew better than to speak to a priest in such a fashion, but it just slipped out.

At once, Sam realized his mistake, apologized, and explained why he did not like Juan Manuel. How *el niño sin piernas* seemed to get anything he wanted. He didn't have the same chores as the other boys and was often allowed to break dorm rules—the staff just looked the other way. But more than that, he bragged about it. "And he is always pounding those drumsticks," Sam said.

I expected the priest to encourage him to have a good relationship with Juan Manuel, giving him a standard line such as, "At NPH, we treat everyone with respect and as a family." But for this meeting, Father Ron just let him talk. I knew Juan Manuel wasn't the sole cause of Sam's anxiety and so did Father Ron. He understood that letting Sam vent about one person would help relieve the pressure and anxiety Sam had been carrying around. And for the first time, I understood the priest's role.

Father Ron knew that the statements, as simple and crass as they were, meant so much more. The conversation was the breakthrough he had hoped and prayed for. The product of weeks of one-sided discussions and long, painful periods of silence.

13

Keep Away
Sam

I FINISHED CLEANING UP the kitchen with my crew and walked toward the main field where several hundred kids were playing. The grounds were constructed with a pavilion at one end. In the middle was a large grassy area circled by the home's buildings. They called it "the field" since most of the time it was used for playing soccer. The open-air pavilion had a back wall with columns surrounding a concrete slab. It was used for gatherings and concerts, but on Saturday evenings, it was transformed into a makeshift church for mass.

I was leaning against a bench in the yard watching an intense soccer match on the field in front of me. The older boys and a few athletic younger kids were entertaining the others as they ran back and forth, bumping the ball with their heads, slide-tackling, and playing like their lives depended on it. The boys knew exactly where to send the ball for their teammates, and somehow, knew who was on their team even though they weren't wearing uniforms. Their camaraderie made me feel like more of an outsider than ever. I had not taken the time to get to know any of them.

A young boy was driving toward the goal, dodging between players, skillfully kicking the ball from one foot to the other. The goalie was hopping back and forth as he approached, trying to stay nimble, ready to dive in either direction. He was the only thing between the boy and the goal. The goalie was big, at least four inches taller than the other players, and much stronger than the ball handler. He stared with determination, and I noticed he watched his opponent's face more than his feet. He could easily overpower the boy but respected his agility and speed. As the distance between them closed, everyone on the sidelines cheered, not for either player, but for the sport. The boy with the ball slowed, enticing his opponent, waiting for the goalie to sweep in and try to stop the ball. When he did, the ballhandler kicked the ball left with the side of his foot and darted past. The goalie was too slow to catch him. As he charged forward, his confidence energized the crowd but when he took his shot, it missed to the left. Throwing up his arms, he fell to the ground as the fans groaned.

I expected anger or frustration, but there was nothing but laughter. Even the girls watching from the sideline were laughing with him. Happiness filled the air. This was such a strange place.

To the east of the field, the *bebes*—the youngest children here—played on an old, green, rickety swing set. Little ones pushing little ones. Older girls watched over them to make sure no one would walk in front of a swinging child and get knocked down or injured.

I turned my attention to the front gate and spent my time making mental notes of who was entering, at what time, how they locked it, and even where Luis kept the key. Luis was the groundskeeper and drove the supply van, coming and going every day. I tried to talk to him once to see if I could get close, but he avoided all the kids. He was a quiet man who went about his work as if the children who lived here didn't exist.

Finding a way out was my only focus. Everything would need to be taken into consideration, and timing was critical. Like before, I had to weigh the challenges of escape. Here, the obstacles were greater because the home was so far away from a city. It would be easy for them to catch me walking alone down a country road.

"Sam, how are you getting on?" Father Ron asked as he approached me from behind. He was always surprising me. Dressed in his holy garments, he was carrying a box with a chalice, Bible, and the other things he used during Mass. "Come and help us."

"Yes, Father," I replied as he handed me the box and I followed him to the pavilion. Jose was standing on the edge of the concrete slab, waiting. He eyed me up and down; not smiling but not angry that I was helping, either. I had noticed the boys here also called him *Blanco*. He didn't seem to care. He always had a smile on his face and a good disposition.

Jose was the assigned server for Mass. Every Saturday night, someone would help Father Ron at the altar, bringing him his chalice and bowls or handing him the Bible. I sat in Mass wondering how anyone knew the timing so well to be able to do things right. The kids at the home said all the prayers by heart and knew what words to repeat. They sang every song and moved in unison when it was time to sit, kneel, or stand. It was like watching a choreographed dance. I was always a second behind, eyeing the kids next to me for signals on what to do next. This week would be no different.

"Sam, do you like our Masses?" Father asked as he straightened a long, narrow piece of fabric that hung around his neck.

"Yes." I knew it was the right answer, but frankly, I had never really thought about it. No one ever asked me what I liked or didn't like.

"Did you find anything interesting in my sermon last week?"

He was testing me, and Jose was smiling. It's not that I didn't hear his words, but I certainly wasn't listening closely. There was so much to watch that I really hadn't absorbed a word of what he said.

"I like the singing," I answered. It was the best way to avoid the quiz.

"Good. I like it too."

He left it at that. As much as I was unsure of him, I was no longer suspicious or scared of his motives. At every turn, he seemed authentic and honest.

"Someday you can be my assistant—we call it a server—at Mass What do you think?"

"I wouldn't know what to do," I replied.

Jose broke in as he began to empty the contents of the box on the altar. "I never went to Mass before coming here," he said. "Father will teach you."

"Perhaps Jose can show you?" Father Ron turned and smiled at Jose. "Do you think you could do that?

"Yes, of course, Padre," he answered without looking at me.

I wasn't sure I would ever want to be in front of all the kids, having everyone's eyes on me. I certainly didn't think Jose would ever help me after what had happened between us, but I nodded my head once to end the conversation.

Twenty minutes before Mass started, Father Ron guided me where to place things on the altar. Soon, he sat down to get ready for the service and I headed for the chairs in the back row of the pavilion.

As I waited, my attention turned to a group of little girls playing at the edge of the concrete. They twirled two jump ropes as one girl hopped quickly from one foot to the other between them and chanted:

A la una, anda la mula
A las dos, tira la coz
A las tres, tira otra vez
A las cuatro, pega un salto
A las cinco, pega un brinco
A las seis, salta como véis
A las siete, salta pronto y vete...

I was amazed at the quick feet of the girl in the center. How did she keep from falling or tripping on the two ropes as they twirled in opposite directions?

My eyes caught an older girl waiting to take a turn. She had her hands on her hips and was looking straight into my eyes. It startled me. Was she mad? Was I staring too long? I wasn't sure, but she was beautiful. It took me a second to glance away.

Jose rang a large bell to let the kids know it was time for Saturday Mass. Like a mob scene, they came running and the chairs began to fill.

Juan Manuel, the boy with no legs, went to the front. He played with the music group and had a special chair by the altar. I noticed that he pulled it forward to be closer to the audience than the rest of the musicians. He hopped up and started strumming on a guitar.

No one had really paid too much attention to me since I arrived. I followed everyone into the dining hall at each meal. I sat near the boys my age but just a few feet away, so I didn't have to talk to them. I watched the others in the dorms to know when I should wash my face or brush my teeth. I went to school at the right time and sat at my desk, watching the teacher, hoping she would never ask me a question. So far, I had been able to avoid contact with everyone, and no one had hurt me.

The only person I talked to regularly besides Father Ron was Anita, a social worker at the home. She met with me on the first day and every Monday afternoon since. She was funny; always carrying a pile of folders that looked ready to fall, looking for glasses that were usually on her head, and accepting my one-word answers. This place didn't seem to worry about getting too deep into my thoughts or pushing me too hard, which was usually what got me into trouble. So, I just kept moving forward, waiting for—or expecting—either the other shoe to drop with Jose, or a chance to run.

One evening, a situation started brewing. I entered the dorm room and walked into the middle of a game of keep away with one of the boy's shoes. Just like in the last orphanage, we shared clothes, but shoes were our own.

In both homes, we threw our dirty laundry into a big pile for washing. At the end of the week, the kids assigned to laundry duty would deliver clean, folded clothes—shirts, shorts, underwear, and socks—sorted in piles on the floor. We would take turns picking out clothes from the pile and putting them in our lockers. Here, no one made a big deal about sharing clothes or who got what each week, unlike the last orphanage, where kids were always fighting over the best T-shirts or shorts with pockets.

The system was fine with me. I kept my shoes in my locker and took whatever was available when I got my turn to choose. Our dorm leader would come through to inspect our lockers and make sure they were in order and our beds were made. Keeping things neat was easy when you had so little.

A boy named Carl had forgotten to put his shoes away, not for the first time. The boys knew keeping the dorm clean was everyone's responsibility. We were instructed to make our beds and keep our clothes and other items picked up. The boys saw this situation as an opportunity to teach Carl a lesson, and he was playing their game, running from boy to boy to get his shoe back. Even Juan Manuel, the boy with no legs, was in on the action. He had hopped up on a bed and was throwing the shoe around with the others. It was amazing how he could move so quickly without legs. I wondered why he was never picked on. In fact, he was often the one doing the bullying.

As Carl's frustration grew, I assumed this "game" would turn into a brawl like these things usually did at the other orphanage. I was preparing to see who would come after me and how I might fight back if they did. I knew being the new guy meant someone would want to test my reaction to a fight, to see what side I'd take and challenge my toughness. Proving yourself that first time can be the difference between a life of persecution or peace and respect.

Just as the game reached maximum intensity, Jose walked into the room. He marched right between the kids playing catch with the shoe, ignoring their little game. He went to his locker and pulled out a book. The boys continued tossing the shoe around and Carl jumped from one end of the room to the other. I stood there, leaning on the corner of my bunk bed, and watched it all play out.

Carl was angry. I could feel the tension rising as he pleaded for the boys to return his shoe. They just laughed at him. One boy grabbed the shoe and hurled it toward Jose. He snatched the shoe out of the air with one hand, without looking, and tossed it back to Carl without any reaction.

"Hey, why did you do that?" one boy yelled.

Jose looked up at him without a word. Then, he looked at me. Did he think I was the instigator?

The rest of the boys quietly went back to their business. *Here it comes,* I thought, *the real fight.* But it didn't. The boys didn't pressure Jose further and simply let the issue die out. Soon, the dinner bell rang, and it was back to our usual routine. At that moment, I realized Jose had everyone's respect. That was why Father Ron liked having Jose as his Mass server: he kept the peace.

14

Running Again
Jorge

SAM WAS STANDING IN line for lunch, and I expected him to be looking ahead to check out the menu. Instead, he was eyeing a girl behind him in line. She was the same girl he had watched jump rope, deliver food trays to the little babies, and tend to the children during Mass. Sitting in the back row, behind everyone, he watched her every move.

His interest reminded me of the first time I laid eyes on Rosa. She was working with her family in the market and I was reluctantly carrying bags for my mother. We had walked for what seemed like miles to the marketplace, ending up at a vegetable stand with my mother arguing with the man about his prices. I was looking around aimlessly when I saw her. Rosa and I locked eyes and were both smiling at the heated battle that we knew was just part of their routine. I remember sensing her kindness and not understanding the feeling that was drawing me in.

For weeks, my mother was perplexed by how quickly I volunteered to go with her to the market. I would try to stay patient while she shopped, secretly urging her to move toward Rosa's family stand. My heart would jump as soon as I saw her in the crowd. I usually saw her before she spotted me. We started to meet at the end of the stand, by the fruit, and talk for the few minutes we could before either her father or my mother moved us along.

Now it was Sam's turn to feel electrified by someone. I was hoping she would be a kind and good person like my Rosa.

He was like a statue holding his tray when she walked towards him. "Hola, Sammy," she said.

I could tell he was trying not to show his feelings as he slowly returned her greeting. "Hola, Eva."

"How did you know my name?" she asked.

"I've been watching you; especially when you're caring for the children," he replied.

"You watch me? What do you see?" she asked.

He hesitated for a moment. "I see the love on their faces, and their love for you."

Sam seemed to have found confidence that I had never seen before, especially with a stranger. He stared right into her eyes.

Two of Eva's friends walked up with their trays and giggled, but not Eva. She just looked straight back at Sam, nodded her head, and walked away.

One evening, Sammy was finishing his chores in the kitchen, spending extra time to make sure everything was put away correctly. He was always a diligent worker. You could count on him to finish a task completely. Tonight, he was stalling.

On Thursday evenings, Olegario, the director of the home, visited his parents in Santa Ana. Sammy knew the routine. Luis would let him out the front gate and shut the latch as if to secure it, but instead, would leave the lock open with the gate barely ajar. Sam discovered it weeks ago. It allowed Olegario to return later without bothering Luis.

As Sam left the kitchen, he strolled across the yard to make sure the car was gone. He wanted enough time for Luis to clear the area.

I wanted to yell at him 'don't run.' I wanted to tell him so many things, but all I could do was watch.

He strolled slowly along the wall, cracked the gate open, and slid right out. I knew no one would notice.

Sammy simply walked up the gravel road by himself. Into the darkness, he breathed a sigh of relief. He felt free. But was this real freedom?

The El Salvador sky was lit with stars and an almost full moon. With no streetlights or a city nearby, it was like walking on another planet. The whole event was much less dramatic than his escape from the last home. But this time, I was more scared than ever because there was nowhere for him to go. Even the boys at the bridge seemed like a refuge from this vast darkness.

Sam walked for about three miles and had less determination than I expected. Eventually, he looked back over his shoulder and decided no one was coming for him, so he took a moment to sit on a big rock in a field. In the distance, he saw the lights of a city. He had picked up a stick along the way and peeled at the bark, pulling the wood apart into small pieces as he considered his next move.

I knew what he was thinking. Should he go to Santa Ana? Should he try to get a ride and go far away? Should he go back? There were no good answers to any of these questions. If only I could talk to him.

There was something peaceful about the way Sam was sitting. He looked up at the stars and enjoyed the quiet, cool breeze on his face. In the air, there was an earthy smell from the soil of the field combined with a faint smell of jasmine. It blossomed in the cool night air and reminded me of a wall of Cestrum jasmine in our old neighborhood. Rosa loved that wall. I envisioned the vines hanging down over the fence, and I could see her close her eyes to take in the beautiful smell as we walked down the street in the evenings, hand in hand.

Sam took the small wooden cross out of his pocket. It was the cross I had given him long ago. He had hung it in his room, and I knew it was left behind at our house when we went on our final, fatal ride. My father had given it back to him in the hospital, and Sam had kept it all this time.

I knew Sam felt alone. There was no one watching over him. I wished he knew I was right there by his side.

For a long time, Sam sat rubbing the cross with his fingers. Then he stood up, took a deep breath, and to my surprise, turned back toward the gates of NPH. It was the first time Sam made his own decision about what he should do with his life. There was freedom knowing he could leave, but power knowing he had the choice to stay.

Sam walked back through the gate the same way he had left, quietly. He looked around with relief.

It wasn't until he got halfway across the field that Jose appeared next to him.

"Out for your nightly stroll?" he asked.

Sam didn't answer.

"Did you find anything interesting out there?" Jose wasn't going to let Sam go without hearing his response.

"No. I guess I didn't, or I wouldn't have come back," Sam said, turning to face Jose.

For a few seconds, the two stood and stared at each other. I wondered if Jose would tell the directors that Sam had tried to run.

Jose was the one to break the ice. "That's a good decision. I guess if you're going to stay here, we may as well head back to the dorms and get some sleep," he said.

Then, Jose smiled, turned, and slowly started walking toward the dorms. Sam followed him. I knew Sam liked him. We both did.

I was sure Sam was curious to see if he was going to say anything, but instead, he asked, "Does it bother you that they call you *Blanco*?"

"Why would it? I *am* blanco compared to the rest of you," he said and laughed.

Sammy couldn't argue. Jose was not easily riled up. It was his way to navigate living in this home.

As they walked into the dorm, someone yelled, "Hey, where have you two been?"

Jose simply shrugged, smiled, and headed to his bed.

15

Having Friends
Sam

BEFORE MASS ON SATURDAY nights, I made it a practice to show up early to help Jose. Together, we would set up the altar and place everything in just the right spot for Father Ron. I loved the feel of the beautiful white altar cloths and the cold metal cups and plates.

Jose had become my friend. I trusted him. He never spoke one word about my escape to anyone, but he didn't want to discuss it with me either. I tried to bring it up once and he simply shut me down.

"This is a good place to call home," he said. "If you leave, that's on you."

It was the thing I liked about him the most, his unwavering loyalty. He was loyal to Father Ron, to NPH, and even, for some unknown reason, to me.

As the weeks passed, Eva and I found ourselves getting to know one another—talking, laughing, and exchanging little gifts. Since Jorge, I hadn't felt a bond with anyone like I did with her. It wasn't just a boy-girl thing. She was truly a friend, someone who cared about me, listened to me, challenged me, and eventually, wanted me to know about her.

I decided to stay at NPH. I told myself in the field it was because of the food and safety; never having to worry about where I would get my next meal. But I was also staying for Eva. She was the first girl who meant anything to me. The first one who ever cared. The first one who might even love me someday.

That's what made it so important, and difficult, to be patient and not push her. I needed to be different from the other boys. And I was. Unlike the others, I didn't brag. I didn't show off in front of the girls or try to act older or tougher than I was.

Over and over, Father Ron's words ran through my mind: "No matter what, Sammy, always treat others and yourself with respect." I didn't always succeed with the boys, but when it came to girls, especially Eva, I was committed to being considerate. I wanted to be like Jorge, remembering how tenderly he had cared for Rosa.

We spent months getting close to one another before Eva and I faced our first challenge as a "couple." She was leaving the orphanage for three weeks with a group of NPH musicians and dancers to perform fiestas in the United States. The night she told me about the trip, my stomach sank. I was already missing her. It was the same sinking feeling I felt in my chest after Jorge died.

The night before the troupe's departure, I was looking for ways to tell her my true feelings. The pending separation made me anxious, feeling like I had to get it out. But once again, I needed to be patient. Otoniel, the director of the NPH music program, had announced at dinner that we had to say our goodbyes to the troupe early because they would have a final, late-night rehearsal in preparation for the trip.

The troupe would leave for the airport at five a.m. and would have no time for long goodbyes.

I waited by a tree outside the cafeteria. Eva and I had worked the dinner cleanup shift but were never alone. I was desperate to give her my gift, but I didn't want the others snooping. It would be my last chance to see her before her evening practice. Three weeks seemed like forever.

The kitchen door swung open and Eva walked through, looking side to side. It made me happy to know she was searching for me too. She smiled when our eyes locked. She met me at the tree and sat down so we could spend our last moments together.

"I hope you have a great trip to the US," I told her.

"No, you don't," she replied. "You want me to be miserable without you."

She was right.

I smiled. She got serious, "I am incredibly nervous about the airplane ride. What if we crash? What if I don't like it there?"

I had the exact same fears. I worried that something bad might happen, and I would never see her again. I decided not to answer.

Instead, I changed the subject. "I…I have a…a gift for you." The words came out choppy and nervous as I held out my fist. It was a small bracelet I made from colored string. It wasn't unique, but it was an important symbol for me.

"I know the trip will be great," I said. "You will meet wonderful people, I'm sure about it." I put the bracelet around her wrist. "You can wear this for strength and so you don't forget about me." She rubbed it with her finger but didn't look at me.

"Thank you, Sammy," she replied quietly as she stood up to leave. "I love it. I will keep it with me always." It was the reaction I'd hoped for, yet I was insecure about us and the separation we were facing.

We walked to her dormitory in silence. I was worried she didn't like the bracelet or maybe that she didn't like me. When we got to her door, she quickly turned and told me, "*Te extrañare.* (I will miss you.)" She kissed me on the lips for the first time, then she was gone.

As I walked away, I could hear girls giggling. Her friends had been watching us from their window, but I didn't bother to look back. It didn't matter. I was so happy—happier than I had been since I could remember.

My excitement got the best of me, and an hour later I snuck out of the dorm. I had to see her just one more time and knew she would be practicing with the others in the pavilion. I hid behind a tree and watched as she danced, concentrating on every step. Everyone wanted to make Otoniel proud.

"What are you doing here?" I felt a hand on my shoulder. "Aren't you supposed to be in your dorm?"

Father Ron knew the answer but before I had a chance to respond, he continued, "I'll walk you back, and we can talk."

Anyone but Father Ron would have punished me for being out of the dorm at that hour. Instead, he explained that he had looked for me in my room, and when I wasn't there, he figured I had snuck out to watch the troupe. I was always amazed by how much he knew about what went on in this place and how deeply he understood each of us.

As we walked across the grass in the dark, he told me he was looking for a special projects assistant and wondered if I was interested in the job. It would require me to greet visitors and run errands. He told me I had made an impression on him, especially with my quiet willingness to help others. He said if I did a good job, I could eventually get my license and be his driver. The whole idea was so exciting I forgot about Eva, the rehearsal, and her trip.

Of course, I said yes.

"I knew I chose the right man for the job," he said as he patted me on the shoulder. Then he did something that had a lasting effect on me. He shook my hand and said, "Thank you, Sammy. I'm looking forward to working with you when I return from the US."

As he walked away, I felt something I hadn't felt in a long time; maybe not since I'd helped Jorge on the bread route, or maybe never. I felt *proud*, and thanks to Father Ron, for the first time in my life, I felt like a man.

The next few days passed slowly. There was no Saturday Mass No music. No Father Ron or Otoniel. The whole place had a sense of loneliness as if something were missing.

A week later, Olegario announced there would be an outing. This was a first for me, but Jose said they sometimes took the kids on special outings. He said a donor had sponsored the buses and tickets.

We were going to a waterpark called Sihuatehuacán. I had seen these places from a distance while delivering bread but never had any interest. I didn't know how to swim.

In the dorm that evening, the caregivers brought a clean pile of laundry and told us to find shorts that would dry easily so we could use them as swimsuits. None of us had ever owned a swimsuit. I sat on my bed thinking about how I might get out of going.

"Hey, Sam, come get your shorts," one of the boys yelled. The room was buzzing as the boys talked about the pools and waterslides.

The next morning, I found myself standing in line, nervously squeezing a towel as two yellow school buses pulled up in the circle drive. Jose walked up next to me and noticed my anxiety. I was happy that Eva wasn't here to see my face. She would have known at once that something was wrong.

"What's up with you?" he asked.

"Nothing," I replied without looking at him.

"You don't look like someone headed to a waterpark," he said over his shoulder as we got on the bus. I was glad when he plopped down in an empty seat and motioned for me to sit next to him.

After the bus was on the road, I leaned over to him, "I need to tell you something."

"Thinking of running again?" he asked.

"No, nothing like that," I said. Then, I looked around to make sure no one else was listening. "I don't know how to swim."

"Have you ever tried?" he asked.

"I've never been in a pool. The only water I've been in is the river," I said. "When I was living under the bridge, we used the river to bathe and wash our clothes."

"Swimming in a pool is no different than the river," he said.

"I never swam, just stood, and only in water up to my stomach," I replied.

Jose sat for a second, thinking. "Here's what you do. When we get there, don't go near the deep end." He looked around and continued, "The boys love to push people in, and if they know you're afraid of water and can't swim, you will be a target."

That made me more nervous.

"I will stick with you," he continued, "and we will go in the shallow end together. We'll just stand there and talk. Once they start swimming, I'll show you what to do."

The pool was enormous with chairs arranged around a concrete deck. At the far end, there was a huge circular slide with rushing water that dropped kids into the deep end. The kids were so excited about the slide that no one paid any attention as we set our towels down on the opposite end of the pool.

Jose jumped in and I watched as he stood up in the water. It was only as deep as his chest. I sat on the side of the pool and eased myself in. It was a wonderful relief from the heat of the bus.

While the other kids were busy elbowing each other to climb the stairs of the slide, Jose showed me how to paddle with my hands and lift my feet off the bottom of the pool. Then, he taught me how to hold my breath and plug my nose.

Soon, I was splashing around and moving from one side of the pool to the other. I shook my head to get the water out of my eyes and nose. Jose watched from the line for the waterslide and nodded his approval as I took a break on the deck.

"Hey, Sam," one of the boys yelled. "Why are you in the shallow end? Don't you want to try the slide?"

Jose waved me over. Earlier, he promised to stay with me if I wanted to try the slide. He'd go first and wait at the side of the pool when I came down. Reluctantly, I got up and joined him.

As we waited, he told me what to do after the slide dumped me in the pool. "Hold your breath, let your body float to the top, and paddle to the edge of the pool," he said.

I stood in line on the long, tall ladder, staring up at the top of the slide and watching each kid land and swim back. It looked as if the heavy kids went to the bottom of the pool. At my size, I guessed I would go halfway. There was no worry about the ride itself or the entry into the water; I just didn't want to panic on the swim back to the side of the pool.

When it was my turn, I laid on my back, took a deep breath, and let go, zipping down the curvy slide. Then, I plunged into the water. I didn't realize how silent it would be with my whole body submerged. My ears felt like they were full, but it was quiet and peaceful. I froze and realized my body was slowly rising toward the surface just like Jose said.

I popped up on the surface and gasped a huge breath before paddling like crazy. A few of the kids laughed at my splashy swim stroke, but I made it to the ladder. Jose stood at the side of the pool, watching me with a smile. He nodded and went to take another turn. And his student followed him, this time with confidence.

It was quiet on the bus ride back. Everyone was happy and tired. I watched the landscape passing the windows. Out of habit, I was looking to see if I recognized anything—Diego's house or anyone on the streets. And then it appeared. The small *tienda* with bright yellow metal chairs. I recognized it at once. Jorge and I had been there many times.

The memories came flooding back. The old woman was fat and wore a long dress. She would take our lunch order as we sat at the corner table. Every time we entered the restaurant, she threw her arms out to hug Jorge. I couldn't remember her name, but I recalled her rubbing my head and commenting on my short hair. It was newly cut, and she liked it. On an earlier visit, she had pointed her finger at Jorge and told him I looked messy. We sat outside in those yellow chairs and she brought us *pupusas*. Jorge ordered two, but she always gave us an extra with a smile and a wave of her hand as he protested.

I watched the little restaurant disappear. It hit me that I was calm, looking but not searching. Interested but not anxious. There was no desperation to run or to find something familiar to go back to. I was comfortable at this orphanage: decent food, no beatings, and a simple schedule of activities and chores. I had a friend, Jose, and of course, there was Eva. I felt part of a family. I didn't want to run. NPH had become my home.

16

A Perfect Union
Jorge

THERE IT WAS, the tienda with the yellow chairs; the one where Rosa and I had gone on our first date. Juana was there that first day and every day since. She would never let me forget how lovestruck I was when I laid eyes on Rosa. Over the years, I would stop in with the family or Sam. It was still my favorite place, a place where I was always greeted with open arms.

Juana knew Rosa's family, or at least knew of them, and had a soft spot for them. Rosa had three sisters and a brother. Every week, we would play our cat-and-mouse game at the produce stand, working up the nerve to talk to one another. I remember her sitting on a yellow chair in the restaurant with her older sister, waiting for food. I walked in behind my mother, and finally getting up the nerve, I quietly said, "Hola."

From the beginning, it wasn't her looks that captivated me, it was her quiet resolve. That first encounter, she sat perfectly still, looking into my eyes. No emotion, no playful smile. Simply curious, sizing me up in her mind. What was she thinking? It was a question I would ask myself for years.

Rosa did not wear her heart on her sleeve like other people. She didn't speak unless she had something to say. She watched things unfold and spoke softly.

We met at Juana's restaurant many times. Sometimes, if we had money, we would order one pupusa and share it. Other times, we would sit in the yellow chairs and just talk. Juana never asked us to leave.

I found myself telling her so much, and she listened to every word. After a year, I asked to meet her family. I wanted her father to understand that I would be a good man for her and take care of her forever. I had no idea how, but I was determined to make a good impression and make Rosa mine. I don't know what kind of impression I made in the beginning or if I earned respect by simply hanging around for a long time, but her father took a liking to the idea of us together. It was an easy transition to starting our family.

Our life was simple. I worked any job I could get. I helped my father. I delivered things. I loaded trucks at the plant. It was just enough to allow me and Rosa to move into a small house. And with few material things, we set up a life together.

It was just the two of us when I brought Sam home from the dump, walking into the house with the little bundle in my arms. She listened quietly while I explained how I found him in the trash and that we needed to take him to the hospital to see a doctor. I watched her get a bucket of water, take him from my arms and wash his helpless little body. She gently laid him down and peeled back the dirty blue blanket he had been wrapped in. She pulled off his clothes and slowly, softly washed the filth from the crevices of his body. He was thin and small but kicking and crying like a fighter. She rocked him and tried to feed him, and soon, he fell asleep in her arms.

It was 1989, and the Farabundo Martí National Liberation Front was fighting a civil war. The country had been at war for years. The hospital was a mess and full of people sitting on the floors, lying on gurneys, and yelling at nurses who were running from one patient to another in a futile struggle to keep up. When it was my turn, they looked over the baby and then gave him right back to me. There was no time for social services or paperwork.

"You are taking him home with you?" the nurse nodded. It sounded like a question, but she wasn't asking us; she was telling us and already writing my answer on the clipboard before I could respond. Then, she was gone, running out the door to the next patient. If I was willing, they were happy to let me take him home.

For days, I watched Rosa care for him. She didn't question if we planned to keep him. She didn't ask what the doctors had said about his future. I explained the stomach issues they had told me about and handed her the bottle of medicine the doctor had given me. But that was it. I didn't have any other information.

In the evenings, I sat across from them in silence as Rosa fed and rocked him. There was no need to discuss if we would care for him. It was clear what we had to do. He was now ours, simply because my curiosity had compelled me to check out something I saw moving in the garbage.

17

Back from the U.S.
Sam

THE WEEKS WERE HARD while Eva was away. I kept thinking about our last few minutes together, especially that moment when she kissed me on the lips. I thought about her all the time; during class, on the playground, walking past the girl's dorm. One day, the kids caught me daydreaming in school and pointed me out to the teacher. I was thinking about what things would be like when the bus came bouncing through that gate and we were together again.

I couldn't wait to tell her my good news. I had already registered for driver's education and was reading about how to drive a car. Father Ron said I might be able to get behind the wheel in a few months. The anticipation built all week for everyone in the home.

We were all excited about the group's return. But when they did return, what I expected and what I saw were two different things.

The bus arrived around two in the afternoon. The teachers had canceled afternoon classes, and as soon as we heard the gate, everyone ran out to greet our friends. The singers and dancers got off the two buses, smiling and laughing, everyone hugging. One by one, I watched and waited. I didn't see Eva. Then, after the others had exited, I saw her.

I saw *them*.

She was with Juan Manuel. They were smiling and laughing as they got off the bus together. She was helping him with his bag. And he loved the attention.

Even from a distance, I noticed it. Her wrist was bare. The bracelet was gone. She had promised to wear it. Immediately, I was bitter, thinking about Juan Manuel spending all those days with her, once again getting his way, using the power of sympathy to manipulate. I knew it was wrong to have those thoughts about someone who'd had so many struggles, but I also knew how he played people, and now he had played Eva. I turned and went back to my dorm.

At dinner, Otoniel stood in front of everyone to report on the trip. The entire troupe was asked to line up at the front of the cafeteria as he talked about their wonderful performances, and how well everyone had gotten along with their host families. We all understood it was an important opportunity to connect with the sponsors who helped finance our home. The kids who traveled were proud of their work.

As Otoniel spoke, I couldn't take my eyes off Eva.

"I can't tell you how proud I am of the way this troupe represented NPH," he said, but I barely heard his words. I was too caught up in my own anger and jealousy.

Juan was up front too, twirling his drumsticks. *Show off*, I thought. He was perched on a stool, and as Otoniel talked, Juan took fake bows, trying to get noticed. All eyes were on him, including Eva's, and everyone was laughing.

After dinner, I went to the dishwashing station to do my chores. Eva was in the kitchen too, but I didn't look at her. I avoided her by volunteering to wipe down tables in the cafeteria.

In the far corner, I saw Otoniel and Juan sitting together. Otoniel was holding Juan's drumsticks in one hand, and a green notebook in the other. It looked serious.

I kept my head down but got closer, wiping a nearby table. "The music would be nothing without me. You need my talent." Juan's words matched his attitude, cocky. Otoniel seemed stunned.

Even I was surprised by Juan's words, and for a moment, I stopped wiping the table to listen. Juan noticed. "What are you looking at?" he snapped. I realized how close I had come and hurried off.

I ran to the kitchen. Eva stood there with her hands on her hips. "Why are you ignoring me?" she asked with a scowl on her face.

"Why do you like Juan?" I shot back. "He's not what you think."

"Me, like Juan? What do you mean?" She started laughing.

"You're not wearing my bracelet."

"Do you mean *my* bracelet?" she said as she pulled it from her pocket. Then, she turned and stormed away. I realized I had been wrong and chased her out the door, yelling her name. I caught up to her, apologizing over and over for my behavior.

"I just misunderstood when I saw you coming off the bus together," I explained.

After a moment, she gave me a playful push on my chest.

"Have you gone crazy without me?" she asked with a smile.

"Tell me about the trip," I said, and for the next hour, we sat on the grass outside the mess hall and talked, about her experiences in the US, my new job, and us. Before I knew it, we were friends again.

I was wrong about Eva. She never liked Juan, but she didn't dislike him either. Just like the others, she felt sorry for him. I wasn't sure that was how he saw their relationship, but I didn't care. She liked me, and that was all that mattered. It made me think. *What was wrong with me that I had such terrible feelings toward Juan?*

I was so happy walking back to my dorm later that evening, I almost didn't see him. Juan was sitting outside, under a tree without his legs. He was alone, writing in the green notebook Otoniel had given him in the mess hall. He never looked up at me, just kept scribbling. I wondered what he was doing, and if it was his punishment.

18

The Driver
Jorge

SAM WAS DRIVING. LIKE any parent or loved one, the shocking realization of time hits when you see a child reaching milestones, especially one as big as driving a car. How had he gotten here? When had he become old enough to drive? Maybe because I was frozen in time, walking through the world unseen, I expected Sam would always be a young boy.

Father Ron had given Sam the task of driving the NPH car for church visits and community outreach events. I had watched Sam go from a boy constantly ready to run away to a man contributing to a vibrant family. I couldn't have imagined this transformation. Though we weren't connected by blood, I was as proud as any father on earth.

Who would have dreamed there would be a place like this? Happy, lively orphans cared for by complete strangers. A home focused on raising children; centered on love, discipline, and respect. The love here was clear and abundant.

The founder of NPH, Father William Wasson, was scheduled to visit and the place was buzzing, anticipating his arrival from Mexico. Things were being painted and cleaned. Father Ron's Saturday evening sermons were themed around the good works of Father

Wasson, including the story of how he started NPH in Mexico. The older kids told their own stories about him to the new kids who had never met him. The reverence for this priest, the one responsible for their home, and the understanding of his core principles were clear to the kids, the staff, and the volunteers. Even Father Ron, who was always calm, seemed nervous and excited.

Father Ron sat in the passenger seat as Sam drove. They were on their way to pick up Father Wasson at the airport. Sam waited in the parking lot by the car, standing on his tiptoes to get a first glimpse of Father Wasson as he and Father Ron exited the sliding glass doors of the airport terminal. Together, they appeared and slowly walked to the car. Sam ran over to take Father Wasson's luggage and lift it into the trunk.

Instead of getting in the car, Father Wasson followed Sam and waited to greet him once the trunk was closed.

"So, you are Samuel?" he asked.

"*Si, Padre*," Sam replied.

Father Wasson spent the next few minutes asking Sam questions: "How long have you been at NPH? Where did you come from? Do you have a family?"

I liked the way he took the time to get to know Sam. He was curious about every little piece of Sam's story, and it was nice that he could talk to Sam without distraction or interruption as they slowly made their way out of the airport parking lot.

During the drive, Father Wasson sat in the back seat commenting on the beauty of El Salvador. Father Ron gave him a report on the five NPH locations in Central America.

Somewhere along the ride, Father Ron began to tell Father Wasson about an opportunity for Juan Manuel. He explained that a doctor in the United States was offering a grant to fix his cleft palate. It would take a series of surgeries, but the costs for the hospital, doctor, and travel would be donated. Juan would have to go to Chicago for the procedures.

I had no idea where Chicago was, but Father Ron seemed excited at the prospect of having Juan's face repaired. He explained that Shriners Hospital took care of kids, including the costs for hospital stays and all surgeries. The doctors volunteered their time and specialized in this type of surgery.

Father Wasson asked where Juan would stay when he was not in the hospital. Who would help with his recovery?

Father Ron explained that another priest, Father Don Headley, was talking to potential host families in Chicago. Juan would stay with them to recover until he was released to fly back to El Salvador. They knew about Juan and had agreed to help.

I never believed there were people like this in the world—people who dedicated their lives to help complete strangers. Father Ron. Father Wasson. The doctors they talked about. No one had ever helped me or anyone in my family. In fact, everyone I knew had been a victim of terrible circumstances, like the *banditos* that robbed and shot Sam and me.

Father Wasson sat quietly for a time, just looking out the window. It was uncomfortable for Sam and Father Ron and they stole glances at each other, wondering what was happening.

Eventually, Father Wasson said, "This is God's will. It should be done."

Did this priest have some sort of vision? I wondered. *Was he able to communicate with God? Did God see me?*

"Thank you," Father Ron replied and relaxed in his seat.

After another long, uncomfortable silence, Father Wasson concluded the conversation about Juan. "He should not go alone," was all he said as the car bounced along the bumpy road leading to the NPH gates.

I could see the surprise on Father Ron's face, but there was no time to respond as 476 kids were screaming and waving flags, expecting Father Wasson's arrival.

19

Off to the U.S.

Sam

LUIS DROVE US TO the airport and popped the trunk as a sign for me to unload our bags. As he pulled away into traffic, I felt a rock in the pit of my stomach. I watched until the car was out of sight, and then followed Juan through the terminal doors. A man jumped ahead to hold open the door for us. When Juan wanted to, he could be very charming and people were compelled to help him. But as soon as he got what he wanted, he moved on, forgetting the kindness he'd been shown.

I gave him credit. He knew how to play the game. So why did it bother me? I was jealous. I realized how wrong it was to feel that way. Juan had endured major setbacks and tragedies in his life, some of which were obvious just by looking at him. Yet, I couldn't shake my dislike for him, or at least, for the way he manipulated people and situations.

Olegario had instructed me to be helpful and polite to everyone during the trip. He didn't know my real feelings about Juan. Even Father Ron believed things were much better between the two of us. I promised Eva I would try to be nicer to him. She seemed to like him.

I tried to concentrate on our surroundings and the experience as we checked in for the flight and boarded the plane. I loaded our bags above the seats and stuffed my small shoulder bag under the seat in front of me. Leaning back, I was terrified. I remembered Eva telling me she was afraid of the plane before her trip. I had consoled and encouraged her then. I never thought I would fly on a plane. Now, I was sitting like a statue, my eyes closed tightly as I gripped both armrests. Terrified.

It wasn't until after takeoff that I could open my eyes again. I glanced over at Juan who was staring out the window. How could he be so calm? The airplane was shaky and bumpy, and it felt like it was about to fall apart. How could something this big get off the ground? I was sure we were going to crash.

Juan was turned sideways toward the window, relaxed, enjoying the twists and turns of takeoff. As I looked over at him, the ground disappeared and it made my chest tighten. The plane tilted again, and it seemed like the ground was coming through the window. I just wanted to be back at NPH. It seemed funny that not long ago I was planning my escape.

Beyond my fear of flying, I never wanted any of this. I recalled how Olegario and Father Ron talked me into—actually, *forced* me into—going to Chicago with Juan.

I was eating breakfast one morning when Anita, the NPH social worker, told me to go to Olegario's office when I finished. And when Olegario called you to his office "to talk," it was never a good thing. As I washed breakfast dishes, I tried to figure out what I had done wrong. The last time I was in trouble and sent to his office, I had been caught breaking into the supply shed and stealing food with three boys. That was two years ago. At that time, Olegario was extremely angry and made us promise to never do anything like that again. I hadn't. I wasn't even hanging out with the same guys anymore to make sure I didn't get caught up in their antics. I liked it here and, like Jose, I wanted to stay. The thought of being sent back to the old orphanage was always on my mind. Olegario and Father

Ron told me that would never happen; I was part of "*la familia*" (the family). Yet for some reason, I didn't believe them.

I walked slowly to Olegario's office and sat down in the chair in front of his desk. When he entered, he was smiling, which was strange.

"Sam, I have something important to discuss with you," he said. He explained that I had been chosen to go with Juan Manuel to the United States, to Chicago, wherever that was. He told me it was a wonderful opportunity. I could practice my English. I could see a new country. I could meet new people and represent NPH.

I sat respectfully and listened as it all came rushing at me. When he was done, I sat quietly. Staring straight ahead, I said, "I don't want to go."

My comment confused Olegario. I couldn't tell him the real reasons why I didn't want to go: I didn't like Juan Manuel. I didn't want to leave the only place I felt comfortable. I would miss Eva. I also didn't think I would like the people in the US. I didn't share any of that. I simply said, "Maybe someone else should go."

Olegario wasn't happy. He told me to think about it and asked me to come back in three days. He wanted me to go to the library and read about the U.S. and Chicago. He told me to ask the kids from the music troupe to share their stories from the fiesta tour.

Eva was the only one I spoke to about the meeting. She loved the idea and started telling me every detail about her time on the fiesta trip. I had to admit her stories about each family and every event piqued my interest.

Over the next few days, Father Ron "ran into" me several times. I knew he was searching for me on purpose—in school, on the grounds, as I worked in the cafeteria—to talk me into going with Juan. He sat with me, presenting the details of the trip, the families, and the things I would see. When I returned to Olegario's office, I reluctantly said yes. I knew it would make both Father Ron and Eva happy. Not that I cared much, but it would be a good thing to do for Juan Manuel.

So, there I was, on an airplane, headed to Chicago. I was supposed to be happy, even excited. Other *pequeños* would have been since it was November, and I was missing my classes. But all I could think about was going to a strange house, speaking their language, eating their food, waiting on Juan, and missing Eva. "Someday, I will have control of my own life," I whispered to myself as I tried to push down the fear and anxiety of the airplane ride. I was reminded of that night in the field, sitting on the rock, the night I decided to stay at NPH.

I noticed something that brought me out of my daydream. A woman, a flight attendant, was pushing a cart down the aisle. What was that for? No one else paid any attention to it. I could see her and the other flight attendants giving food and drinks to the passengers. I didn't want to spend the money Olegario had given me, so I said no when the woman asked if I wanted anything. Juan took a Coke, and she gave him snacks, too. She was gone before I realized the drinks and snacks were free. I should have asked Juan how all this worked, but I didn't like the idea of him telling me how to do things. He would be cocky. Juan loved it when he knew something someone else didn't.

I looked behind me, down the aisle. I was thirsty and wondered if they would come through again.

About four hours into the flight, I heard a "ding" as the pilot came on and said something I didn't quite understand. The flight attendants went up and down the aisle, looking at our seat belts. I had no idea what it meant but soon found myself grabbing the seat again. The plane was shaking, and I was sure we were in trouble. My stomach was rolling. Juan had fallen asleep and didn't even notice. How could he sleep through this disaster? I didn't want to die, and certainly didn't want Juan to be the last person I ever saw. If I woke him, he would know I was afraid. None of the other passengers seemed scared.

In the dark, the lights of Chicago appeared out the window. They formed perfect squares in the distance and seemed to go on forever.

I had no idea if we were crashing or landing, and I was so tense, my shoulders hurt. Juan Manuel finally woke and sat up to stare out the window, and take in the whole experience. The ground came closer and closer. When we hit the runway, I was sure the plane would explode.

Juan was putting on his legs and getting his crutches from under the seat as the plane drove down the runway toward a huge building. I helped him without saying a word. His legs were heavy and hard to retrieve. His polio crutches were always getting tangled. At that moment, I felt sympathy for all Juan had to endure. He pulled each leg on under his shorts, then pulled his sweatpants over them.

Juan had a small, green bag with strings that went around his shoulders. In it, he was supposed to keep his passport and papers, but I noticed he had crammed these documents in the side pocket of his pants. He was stuffing his green notebook in the bag as people started to get off the plane.

We were seated in one of the last rows, so I looked down the aisle to see what the other passengers were doing as they prepared to leave. Most were getting their luggage down, so I did the same and sat back in my seat to wait.

"We will get off the plane last," Juan said as though he'd done this a thousand times.

As we exited the plane, the crew smiled at Juan Manuel as he walked by on his crutches. A woman in a black vest with a badge around her neck was waiting for us with a wheelchair.

"Juan Manuel?" she asked, and then spoke in Spanish. "I'm Joanna, and I'll take you to customs and baggage claim."

Juan Manuel plopped down in the wheelchair and laid his crutches across his lap. I followed as she pushed him up the jetway, relieved to be on the ground and to hear someone speaking Spanish. I understood everything, and it helped me relax. On the way to customs, I remembered Father Ron telling me how we would need to show our passports to the officers before we went to baggage claim.

My job was to take care of the luggage. The slip she held said that there would be a family to meet us. It must be the Byrnes that Olegario and Father Ron told us about. I hoped they would be there. I hoped they would be nice. I hoped they knew that Juan could be...well, Juan.

We walked through O'Hare airport, and I was amazed that there were so many restaurants—everything from coffee shops to fast-food places with big areas where people could sit and eat, talk, work, or read. I had never seen anything like it. The smells made me realize I was hungry, but I knew I shouldn't eat. My stomach was still rolling and making noises from the plane ride. I swallowed hard and hoped things would settle down now that we were safely on the ground.

After customs, Joanna took us to baggage claim. The elevator doors opened slowly, and the only person standing there was a skinny little white boy. He stared straight at us and yelled in English, "Here they are, Dad!" Then he turned and ran away. It made me laugh.

Joanna pushed forward, and when we turned the corner, we saw four adults waiting with the little boy. He was talking fast, and I could tell he was excited. Two of the adults looked like they could have been my parents' age. I always wondered what my parents looked like. How did my mom look when she smiled? Did I look like my dad? The other two people were older, like grandparents.

"I recognized them right away, Dad," the little boy said. "That was the elevator I thought they would use. Their bags should be on carousel number three." And then he ran off again.

Juan Manuel rode in the wheelchair, a single polio crutch sitting on top of the green backpack in his lap. I had picked up the other crutch when it fell off on our walk through the airport. Joanna pushed the wheelchair toward them.

The older woman came to us first. "Hola. I am Mary Jo. We are so glad you're here," she said with a smile, which made me feel good. Then, she leaned over to hug Juan. He had met them at the fiesta and again on their visit to El Salvador. They were friends with Otoniel, the music director. I had not been to Chicago, and I didn't mix with the U.S. visitors when they came to visit us at NPH. I spent that day in my dorm and only saw the guests at lunch or when they toured the dorm building.

A tall man walked over and held out his hand to us. "Hola, Juan. Hola, Samuel. Me llamo Brian."

The older man followed, and after shaking hands with Juan, he grabbed my hand and arm. "How was the flight? I'm Mel." I liked him right away.

"Bumps. I not like it," was all I could say. My stomach was getting worse. The two men laughed.

"Well, it's no wonder. It's windy tonight," said the younger woman. She was keeping an eye on the little boy. "I'm Marlene." She shook both our hands and then motioned for us to follow the boy. "That's Matthew, our son. He's extremely excited to have you stay with us."

Once we collected our bags, we loaded into a van. Brian drove on highways and streets that were bigger and busier than I had ever seen. I sat in the third row with Matthew. Although I spoke some English, he was talking so fast, I was having trouble understanding. I was also distracted by the sights of the city. It was late, well after dark, but the streets were lit up. There were so many people walking around. At gas stations. Coming out of restaurants. No one seemed scared. Cars were everywhere. This was even bigger than San Salvador.

After a while, we arrived at a big house with grass and flowers in the yard. A streetlight lit up the driveway as we unloaded the luggage. I carried Juan's big bag through the front door and turned to set it down when something cold and wet touched the back of my leg. I jumped, letting out a squeal. It was the biggest dog I had ever seen. He jumped back too, and Marlene grabbed his collar.

"This is Murphy. He's friendly," she said, but I was scared. He put his nose up to my leg to smell me, and I reached out to touch the top of his head. His fur was soft on my fingers.

Everyone came in the door, talking all at once. I couldn't take my eyes off the dog who had moved around us to sniff our bags. Matt was the only one who noticed my fear. "He's really nice," he said as he put his arms around the dog's neck.

Marlene introduced us to Maggie, who was younger than Matt and in her pajamas on the couch with another girl, a neighbor who had stayed with Maggie while the rest came to pick us up.

I was surprised when the older couple said goodbye. I assumed they lived here. The house seemed big enough for everyone.

As Brian showed us the upstairs bedroom and bathroom, I kept a watchful eye on the dog. He sniffed everything and walked into the bathroom, moving between us to get next to Brian. When he left the bathroom, he headed back toward our bags. I was sure he would chew something.

As I started to relax (for the first time all day), I looked around the room. There was a big bed with a headboard against the wall and a smaller mattress in the opposite corner on the floor. Both beds were made up with nice blankets and pillows. There was a chair in the corner and a dresser sat next to it. The bathroom was connected to the bedroom. Could it be just for us? It had a single shower, and there was shampoo and soap on a rack inside with towels folded on the shelf.

Brian was showing us how to turn on the water. I wasn't really listening. He opened a cabinet that had deodorant, toothpaste, and other bottles lined up.

"You can hang your towels on this rack when they are wet," he said. "For the shower, turn the knobs like you do on a sink. It takes a while for it to get warm, so it's a good idea to start the water before you get in and then adjust it to the temperature you want."

I couldn't understand all of what he was saying, but I watched and nodded.

As Brian started to leave with Matt, he turned and said, "Oh yeah, remember that here in the states you can put your toilet paper in the toilet. Okay?"

That I understood. Father Ron had given us those instructions, explaining the plumbing in El Salvador could not take paper, but here it could. As he left, I turned around to see Murphy sitting next to our bags. I wasn't sure what to do. I looked at Juan. He had already plopped down on the big bed. "This one is mine, you take the one on the floor," he said.

I wasn't about to argue, so I just nodded. I couldn't stop staring at the huge dog, who walked over to lie on my mattress on the floor. "What should I do?" I asked Juan.

"Come here, boy!" Juan said, and Murphy went right to him. Juan put his face on Murphy's head like they were old friends. I was frozen and all I could think was, *Are you crazy? This beast is going to bite your head off!*

"Murphy!" The call came from downstairs. The dog jumped up and ran toward the voice. "Is he up there?" Marlene asked.

"Yes," Juan Manuel answered and started laughing. He relaxed back on the big pillows against the headboard and opened his green notebook. One thing that amazed me about Juan was his ability to get comfortable in any situation. I tried to relax and began to unpack. I put my folded clothes in piles on top of my suitcase. I set my extra shoes in line with the wall. I took my toothbrush and paste to the bathroom and put them on the counter.

That night, I lay awake wishing I could talk to Eva. I missed her, and I missed home. *Home?* I never thought I would call NPH my home. I remembered how Father Ron tried to get me to talk. It seemed like a lifetime ago. I didn't want to like him. But now, thinking about NPH and Father Ron made me smile. He was my friend, someone I trusted. I knew he thought this was an opportunity, something that would help me as well as Juan. But at that moment, in a strange bed, in a strange house, in a strange country, it didn't feel that way. I sat up and went to the window. We were on the second floor of the house, and I could see rooftops. It was bright on the street; large lights were shining on the blacktop. Even the sky looked brighter than back home. I pushed the curtain open and went back to lie on the mattress and stare at the sky, the same sky that hung above NPH, but different in so many ways. I wondered what everyone was doing back home.

The next morning, Juan was sleeping but I had been awake for over an hour. I was so hungry. I realized I hadn't eaten anything since we left NPH early yesterday. Marlene had offered us food after we arrived, but when I looked at the sandwiches, my stomach jumped, still unsettled from the airplane ride, and thought it would be better if I didn't eat.

I smelled food cooking and decided to go downstairs without Juan. I got dressed and crept down the staircase to the kitchen. Everything in this place was so nice, much nicer than any place I'd ever lived. Marlene was at the stove, and I sat on a chair at the counter.

I didn't think she heard me enter the kitchen and was surprised when she said, "Good morning, Samuel." Without turning around, she asked, "Are you hungry?"

"*Sí*, yes," I said, and she set down a plate of eggs, sausages, and toast. I ate everything.

"Coffee?"

"Yes ... please."

Marlene asked me questions that I politely tried to answer in English. I noticed Matt and Maggie watching TV. They came to the kitchen to eat too, but as soon as I finished, I put my plate in the sink and headed back upstairs. They seemed nice, but I didn't know what to do. And I didn't want to bother them.

20

Room 122

Sam

OVER THE NEXT FEW days, the weather turned cold, like nothing imaginable in El Salvador. Marlene had given us winter coats to wear outside. I didn't love the cold, but there was something fascinating about seeing your breath in the air. I would get out of the car holding my breath and let out a big sigh just to see the white puff in front of me.

I was staying with Brian and Marlene but going to doctors' appointments with Mel and Mary Jo. In the past week, I found out the two couples met each other during a visit to NPH El Salvador, which is ironic since they lived about five blocks apart in Chicago. They had been part of the group from the United States that visited the orphanage. Most were sponsors of children and came to visit. Others were there for a board member meeting.

While they were visiting, Father Ron had the idea to have them work together in caring for Juan while he was having surgery in Chicago. They were an unlikely foursome. Mel and Mary Jo, older with adult children. Brian and Marlene, with two young children.

We left early for the hospital. Marlene and Mary Jo both seemed anxious as we went to the hospital for Juan's first surgery. I was excited to get started. The sooner Juan recovered, the sooner I could go home.

As we entered through the hospital's sliding glass doors, I got distracted and hit both sides of the door frame with Juan's crutches. Carrying them was my job. Juan was quiet and nervous as someone from the hospital pushed him in a wheelchair toward the front desk.

The inside of this building didn't look like any hospital I had ever seen. The lobby smelled nice and had beautiful couches arranged in groups on carpeting with crazy, colorful designs. There were toys, books, and a tree with pictures clipped to the branches—photos of smiling children with staff members.

I followed the rest of the group as we walked through a large lobby to a big front desk. The sign above it read, "Welcome to Shriners' Hospital." It was early, so the lobby was empty, but there was a sense of energy in the building. Even without another soul in the chairs or at any of the tables, it felt like the place was ready for children and activity.

An old man walked toward us. He was wearing a hat that looked like a red box with a yellow tassel hanging off to one side.

"I'm Robert," he said, smiling as he extended a hand. "And who is this?" He focused on Juan, who didn't respond. I could tell Juan was nervous, and his expression was blank. His silence was my cue to speak.

"This is Juan Manuel Pineda," I said with as much confidence as I could muster.

Juan followed up with a simple, "Hello."

"Well, welcome to Shriners. I'll be your guide and show you to Juan's room," Robert said. He turned and signaled for us to follow.

I wondered about the funny hat. Was that so we wouldn't lose him on the way to Juan's room? In the hallway, I saw others wearing them. I stopped trying to figure it out and decided I'd ask Brian later.

We followed Robert down a hallway to an open balcony. Everything at Shriners was big and felt unlike a medical center; it was more like a hotel. Other hospitals smelled like sanitizers. Here, the air smelled fresh. Brian and Marlene seemed impressed too.

Robert stopped at a railing that overlooked a large area with a basketball court, ping pong tables, indoor playground equipment, and games.

"This is where the kids come to have some fun when they start to recover and feel better," he explained, and then looked at me. "Or where their friends and family can pass the time."

The area had two-story windows and large doors that opened to an outdoor sports area just as big as the indoor one. It was late November and leaves had fallen, covering the ground with colors. The leaves left on the trees and shrubs were orange and red, and the green grass was perfectly manicured.

"This place is amazing," Brian said. He told Robert about Matt and Maggie as they walked on. I stood staring over the railing, catching up as they turned a corner to another hallway.

"Juan and your whole family can use anything in the place," Robert said. He turned to talk to two nurses who joked with him and said hello to us. "The cafeteria is just down that hall. Please remember that everything, even for visitors, is free." Robert walked a step ahead, talking to us over his shoulder.

"Here we are, room 122," he said, motioning us in. "I will leave you now, but please stop any of us if you need assistance while you are here," he said. Could I be right? They wore funny hats so they'd be easy to find if we had questions.

Juan's room was like a beautiful bedroom. It had two beds, two closets, two chairs, and a big television hanging from the wall. Luckily for us, the other bed was empty, so we could occupy the whole space. I started putting Juan's things away. Juan sat on the bed and removed his legs. I put the crutches away and then took his legs to the closet one at a time.

If I ever needed medical care, I hoped it could be at a place like this. Even the sounds were nice. The nurses walking by were laughing and talking. Everyone said hello, and they knew the patients by name.

I would learn later that "Shriners" is not just the name of the hospital, but a group of people dedicated to caring for the less fortunate, especially children who suffer from burns and terrible diseases. The Shriners system takes care of kids for free, donating their money and volunteering time to care for children when no one else would. It made me think of Father Wasson, the priest who founded NPH. These people were like him.

Suddenly, a doctor entered the room. He moved quickly and talked fast. "Good morning," he said with a smile. "I am Doctor Patel."

He went to Juan, which I liked. Sometimes, it felt like the adults in our lives were talking around us instead of to us. But Doctor Patel was different. His focus was on Juan, and it made both of us happy. Behind him was a beautiful, young Latina nurse. When I saw her, I stood up a little taller.

"Margarita is here to help translate if there are any questions," the doctor said. His voice was soft and kind.

"Hola, Juan," Margarita said, and then smiled and nodded toward me.

Doctor Patel grabbed a chair, dragging it across the room to where Juan sat in the wheelchair. "I will be Juan's doctor along with David Reisberg," he said.

Then Mary Jo chimed in. "We met you at Juan's intake appointment," she said. "We are his host families."

"Good. You'll be an important part of his recovery," said the doctor as he shook her hand.

He placed the chair in front of Juan and sat down so they were face to face. As he began describing the steps of the surgeries, I was impressed with how he explained things. He gave details, yet the descriptions, with Margarita's translation in Spanish, were simple enough to understand. Doctor Patel never took his eyes off Juan. We just listened. Even Mary Jo and Marlene, who usually had a lot of questions, remained quiet.

When Doctor Patel was talking, it seemed like Juan was the only thing on his mind. I noticed nurses lining up outside the door, waiting for him with charts for other patients but he never flinched. He wasn't rushing his explanation. When he was finished, he answered questions, and then he was out the door, taking paperwork from the first nurse in line as they all followed.

Father Ron had told me Juan's first procedure in his two-year journey would involve taking bone from his hip and using it to rebuild the roof of his mouth. That's what Doctor Patel was explaining to Juan. He talked about the procedure, the incision, and the recovery. It all sounded awful. For the first time, I felt sorry for Juan.

After Doctor Patel left, Margarita took over, reexplaining everything in both English and Spanish. She told Marlene and Mary Jo that the host families would need to bring Juan dinner every evening from the cafeteria, wash his bedding and clothes, and play a vital role in his recovery. *Maybe this place isn't so great after all.* I thought. *Why didn't the hospital staff bring him food? Is this how all U.S. hospitals operate?*

That evening, I was alone in our upstairs bedroom, thinking about Juan's first night in the hospital. Was he scared? Did he miss me? Could he sleep?

Murphy's head peaked around the corner of the door. He didn't enter, just stood there, waiting. Could he sense my fear? Did he know I was feeling alone?

We sat staring at each other for a moment, and then he slowly walked over to me. He turned to face the door and sat down with his back to me. I slid my hand down his back, feeling his soft fur. It was comforting. We sat together for a few minutes before he left the room and walked back downstairs.

The next morning, we all gathered in Juan's room to say our goodbyes before he was wheeled away. The surgery took more than four hours. The chairs in the waiting room were stiff, and all we could do was watch TV. After a while, I asked if I could walk around the hospital. I found the large area with the ping pong table empty and started playing around by myself. When a family entered, I set the paddle down and quietly left.

Everything had gone well, Doctor Patel said. He entered the waiting area still wearing his surgical clothes. He was excited as he explained everything to Mary Jo and Marlene. Juan's recovery looked positive. When he finished, he was out the door and on to his next patient. A nurse with a pile of charts went past the waiting room door, chasing after him.

We went to get food in the cafeteria and then waited for what seemed like forever for Juan to be moved back to his room. Marlene said he had to stay in the recovery area until he was fully awake and stable.

Mary Jo was busy asking me questions. How did I get to NPH? Did I have siblings? Did I like school? Would I go on to university? What did I want to study?

People who have never had to worry about their next meal ask these kinds of questions. The most truthful answer was, "I don't know." I didn't think about these things. In my life, being safe and fed was enough.

Finally, Juan was rolled into the room in his bed, looking miserable. He was in obvious pain. His whole face was swollen and red. Talking hurt him, so he just nodded or shook his head to answer questions. There were ice packs on both cheeks. I imagined they were helpful, but not comfortable. He kept the blanket folded back off his hip where a bandage was covering an incision. It was the spot where they had removed a piece of bone to reconstruct the roof of his mouth.

Mary Jo did the talking, telling him things had gone well and he was doing great. Marlene had her hand on his forearm, looking like she might start crying at any moment.

After an hour, the nurse came to offer a final update on the surgery and said we should go home until the following morning.

At the Byrne's house, there was always something to eat, not just at mealtime, but anytime. Marlene had said we could grab snacks whenever we wanted. Of course, that meant Juan and I were taking snacks up to our bedroom all day and night.

With Juan in the hospital, I had time alone. Every day was the same. I would go to the hospital with Mel and Mary Jo and spend the morning sitting in Juan's room. In the afternoon, they would drop me off at Marlene and Brian's house, and I would sit in the family room watching the Spanish channel—mostly soap operas—and eat snacks. It was quiet with the kids at school, and I liked having the place to myself.

In the evenings, I'd return to the hospital with Brian or Marlene.

21

Car Time
Jorge

My body felt as if I were a passenger on the plane. Sam's fear was my fear too. I shared the feeling of the pit in his stomach. How was it that I could feel the flutters on takeoff? How did I sense the paralyzing fear in his chest during the landing? I don't know. But it all affected me just like it did him.

Getting to the house was a relief. They had made the accommodations comfortable and welcoming, yet everything was unfamiliar.

For the next three weeks at the Byrne house, Sam remained polite and quiet. Marlene worked hard to get conversations going, but Sam kept his distance. The only time he felt relaxed was when he was alone, watching TV or talking to Maggie. She provided a feeling of home, like being with the children of NPH.

Marlene explained that Boris and Javier, *pequeños* from the home, had been their guests during the NPH fiesta. Together, they looked at photos of the events. One showed Boris laughing as he juggled for the kids at a school. Sam knew of both boys, but because they weren't in his dorm, he didn't know them well. In each picture, he searched for Eva and finally found one where she was dancing in the background.

The days passed with Sam going to the hospital and Juan's face slowly healing, the red bruising fading to a light purple and then green. His swollen cheeks slowly returning to normal size.

Finally, it was time to return home to NPH. Sam was thrilled. He said goodbye to Mel, Mary Jo, Brian, Marlene, the kids, and Murphy. He took gifts to Boris and Javier from the Byrne family. Although he told them he would see everyone next time, he felt confident he would never return.

The whole time he was away, Sam dreamed of this night; the night he returned to NPH.

It turned out exactly like his dream. The weather was beautiful, and Eva sat under a tree. He told her stories about the entire trip— from the dog to the hospital and even the food. She listened intently and soaked in every word. It almost made the trip worthwhile.

"Were you afraid of the dog?" she asked.

"No," Sam lied. "He's soft and gentle."

"How was the food? I loved hamburgers," she said.

"I loved the meatloaf," Sam said.

On and on they discussed the trip. Eva related to his "firsts," remembering how she felt on her first airplane ride, her first restaurant, and the first family she stayed with in Minnesota, where they performed before traveling to Chicago.

They laughed and compared stories. Sam made things sound much better than what really occurred. In truth, he had been homesick the whole time, often not sleeping through the night. Yet, the version he told Eva was one of fondness and excitement.

He told those same stories to Father Ron in the car the next day, but this time, there was no animation and much less enthusiasm about the events and interactions with the Byrnes. Sam planned to talk Father Ron into sending someone else on the next trip, but he wasn't quite ready to ask.

"Sam, these trips will get better and more familiar. I know you will eventually look forward to the change of scenery," he said. "This is an important task, but I also want you to enjoy yourself."

Sam was quiet.

"You remember how difficult it was for you to transition to NPH when you first arrived," Father Ron reminded him.

Sam nodded.

"And now, are you happy here?" he asked.

Sam was a bit surprised by the change of subject.

"Yes, *Padre*. I would not want to be anywhere else," he replied. NPH had become his home.

"Yet, you remember that you almost ran away from this place in the middle of the night?"

"How did you—?" Sam was stunned, but before he could finish, Father Ron cut him off.

"We get calls from families up the road when anyone runs away. If they see a *pequeño*, they know to contact me," he explained.

"But no one came for me?" Sam asked.

"Sometimes, it's best for *you* to decide to do the right thing. I made the decision that night to let you figure it out. I knew if we dragged you back here, you would only run again."

"Would you have sent someone after me if I had not turned around?" Sam asked.

Father Ron looked over at Sam, smirking. He had no intention of answering. I loved this about him. He had a way of guiding the children without forcing them.

Then it happened.

BOOM.

The car crashed into the vehicle ahead of them, and the discussion was over. The impact was so hard that both Sam and Father Ron lurched forward, held in only by their seatbelts.

Father Ron turned to Sam, "Are you okay?"

"Yes."

"Stay here." Father Ron got out of the car as Sam sat gripping the steering wheel in shock. The hood of the car was dented upward, and he couldn't see what damage the crash had caused on the other car's rear bumper.

The man in front of them jumped out of his car, yelling, and waving his arms. When he saw Father Ron's priest collar, he momentarily stopped in his tracks. He glared at Sam and then walked over to talk to the priest. Father Ron explained the circumstances as he pulled the NPH insurance card from his wallet.

22

Back to the Byrnes
Sam

SLEDDING IN THE SNOW was something I would never be able to explain to the kids at NPH. How do you describe the soft snow, packed down like sand and forming an icy, smooth track, to people who lived on the equator? First, it was soft and fluffy. Cool but not cold. Then it was packed down and became hard, smooth, and extremely slippery.

Marlene had bundled everyone up in heavy socks, boots, hats, and gloves. She made a custom pair of snow pants for Juan by cutting off the legs and sewing the openings closed so the pants would cover his stumps—there was no way to use his crutches and prosthetic legs on a sledding hill. When we left the house, we looked like aliens. I had never worn so much clothing at one time, and I could barely move or bend my legs under all the layers.

But none of that mattered after my first ride down the hill. Matt went first, showing us how to lie on the sled and hold the handles. It wasn't the best training, as Juan went sideways on his first try, eventually falling off the sled and rolling most of the way down. Marlene ran over to Juan and found him laughing so hard he couldn't even sit up.

I went flying past them both. Pure exhilaration. For the first time, I enjoyed the chilly wind and the spray of snow on my face.

By the time I reached the bottom, I had completely turned around, riding down the hill backward, and landed in a huge snowbank.

"Come on," yelled Matt. "Let's go again!" He was already running back up the hill with his sled in hand.

I didn't realize how cold my body was until we were in the car on the way home. My toes felt hard, and they ached. I had never felt like this. I pulled off my gloves, placing my hands on my cheeks. My face felt cold and hot at the same time; a combination of the frozen snow and burning from the wind.

We arrived home and peeled off our clothes in something Marlene called the "mudroom." Murphy was happy to see us and was eating remnants of snow off the floor before they could melt. Marlene was yanking off boots and laying mittens on the marble fireplace. Everyone was in a good mood.

The conversation about our day together made for a lively dinner. We laughed as we rehashed stories of riding down backward and all the spills we took. Matt bragged about his speed and teased Maggie about screaming all the way down the hill.

Soon we were delivering dirty plates to the kitchen and Marlene was at the sink washing them. I realized that my favorite time was right after dinner. Unlike at the orphanage, there was quiet peace in this house when everyone finished eating.

A few weeks after we arrived, Marlene announced that we were going to eat together each night at six. Juan and I had tried to take our food and eat upstairs but she put a stop to it. Now I was glad she did.

Maggie and I started a ritual of watching a TV show called *Funniest Home Videos* after dinner. It was the perfect show for two people who spoke different languages. But tonight, she was sitting at the snack bar paging through a book, so I plopped down next to her on the kitchen stool.

"What are you doing?" I asked.

"I can't decide which picture to use," she replied. She needed a baby picture of herself for a class project. Next to her sat a large bin of photo albums, and she was flipping through the pages.

I leaned in. "Let me see."

Together we started paging through each book, laughing at the funny poses, crazy expressions, and the hairdos and clothes of Brian and Marlene in their younger days.

"Why did you wear oven mitts on your feet?" I asked, laughing.

"To pretend I was ice skating," she replied and quickly turned the page. "Here I am in the pool."

I pointed to a photo of her with a hose. "You are spraying yourself."

"I was just a baby," she said.

The photos were a collection of the events and times they had shared as a family. It was amazing to see a lifetime of happiness captured in such an organized way. It was something I would never know. There were no photos of my parents because I had no parents. There were no happy times documented with Jorge either. It also meant there were no terrible times captured with Diego or at the first orphanage. Instead, those things were tightly locked up in my memory.

There were photos of Maggie running down the hallway in her diaper, and Brian throwing her in the air. In one picture, she had one leg over the crib, obviously trying to escape. We were both laughing, and I could see Marlene smile as she continued washing the dishes.

"You think this is so funny," Maggie said. "I want to see your baby pictures."

I didn't exactly know what to say. "There are no pictures of me as a baby."

"What? Why not?" she asked.

"No camera. No mother," I said.

"No one ever took a picture of you? Never?"

I could see Marlene out of the corner of my eye. She looked concerned, like Maggie's questions might upset me, but I didn't mind.

Maggie was curious and honestly wanted to know more about me. She didn't judge, and she certainly meant no harm.

"No. There was no way to take a picture," I said. I noticed Marlene had stopped washing the dishes and stood listening from her place at the sink. "The first time anyone took a photograph of me was the day I entered the orphanage. It was for documentation purposes only."

"Why don't you have a family?" Maggie asked.

"I was born sick," I said, not at all embarrassed or hesitant to tell Maggie. "Jorge told me my mom must have been afraid I would get her other kids sick, so she threw me in the garbage."

Marlene was washing the same dish over and over and I noticed her facial expression had changed. She looked sad.

I continued. "I was picked up by a garbage truck and thrown into the local dump."

"You were in the trash? Yuck!" Maggie replied, mesmerized by my story. "How did you get out?"

"A man was there dropping things on the trash pile. He said he saw a little hand and dug to find me wrapped in a blue blanket. To his surprise, I was alive. He carried me home to his wife, and they took me to the hospital. The doctors fixed my stomach problem, and then I lived with the man and his wife."

"What was his name?" she asked.

"Jorge. And his wife's name was Rosa.

"So, you *did* have a family," Maggie said.

"Yes, I guess, for a time." At that moment, I realized Maggie was right. Jorge and Rosa had been my family.

"Jorge was like my dad. But then he was killed," I said.

"How did he die?" she asked. She was locked into my story.

"We were delivering bread. Men robbed us. They shot Jorge, and they shot me too, right here." I touched the scar on the back of my head, and she climbed up to kneel on the stool to get a look at the scar.

Marlene dried her hands and came to look too.

"Jorge drove me to the hospital," I continued. "He died, but I lived."

"Is that when you went to NPH?" Maggie asked.

"No. I went for a bit to live with Jorge's brother, but it was not a good situation, so they sent me to a state orphanage," I said. "Then about ten of us were moved to NPH."

I sat up straight, feeling good that I was able to tell my story to someone.

Without missing a beat, Maggie moved on.

"Okay. Well let's get back to choosing my picture," she said. "I have to take this to school tomorrow."

Marlene walked closer to me and slowly grabbed my hand. I could see a tear running down her cheek. "I am so sorry about Jorge and what happened to you."

23

At Home
Jorge

THE RELATIONSHIP BETWEEN SAM and Maggie reminded me of my girls. How I missed them! Where were they now? Why couldn't I see them? Why was I only able to see Sam?

It was as if my sole purpose were to help him, yet all I could do was watch. I couldn't stop him from stealing. I couldn't stop him from leaving NPH. What was my purpose for being here? It frustrated me.

My girls loved living with Sam. He was funny and entertaining. Without warning, he would grab three items—oranges, rocks, anything small—and juggle for them. They would egg him on to go faster and faster until he dropped the items.

"Where did you learn that?" I asked him one day.

"There was a guy outside the mart who liked to juggle," he said. "When you went in to deliver the bread, I'd sit outside and watch him. He showed me how to throw and told me it was easy, all I had to do was practice. So, I did whenever I got the chance. The key, he told me, is to keep your throws close to your body."

Sam was like that. He would set his mind to something and work at it until he figured it out. For weeks, he walked around throwing two rocks in the air, trying to catch one after the other. I didn't realize what he was doing and never asked. He would toss three rocks and get two or three catches before one throw would be too high or too far away from his body. When he dropped one or more of the rocks, he would start over.

My girls started to notice him practicing. At first, they laughed at him when things fell to the ground, almost hoping he would fail. Soon, they were cheering him on, watching every toss and catch and counting his throws.

As he became more proficient, he would perform for them. It took him a while to connect, both with things and with people, but once he did, he could be a captivating young man.

This same, slow process happened with his host family in Chicago. They were different. This place was different. But Sam was the same. Careful. Guarded. Distant.

The United States was so different from where we lived. It seemed odd to be here, watching Sam with this *gringo* family. Their house was huge, and seeing Sam and Juan lying around felt strange and out of character for what we all were used to. They spoke a different language I shouldn't understand and yet somehow, I did. And although they had different customs and ways of doing just about everything, strangely, it felt like home.

Other things were familiar, like Easter Mass and the rituals of church. Dressing up and sharing the same Eucharist. But their holiday also included big baskets of candy. Juan embraced these unfamiliar traditions, but Sammy remained quiet. I knew he longed for NPH and Eva.

I was the one who had let him down, dying when he needed me. Dying on all of them. Should I have given the thieves all my money? If I had, would they have spared us? What if I had turned the truck around and driven away? Would things have been different?

Yes, I had let him down, and after me, it was Diego. And even my father. Everyone in Sam's life had failed him in one way or another, reinforcing his self-image as a second-class citizen.

Marlene and Brian kept trying to get Sam to open up, asking him questions and attempting to engage him in family activities. When he wasn't around, they'd discuss how to reach him, questioning themselves, hoping they could get through the shell he'd built. They worked so hard to make him comfortable and their intentions were good, but to understand Sam, you needed to understand his past.

There was one glimmer of hope: Maggie. She was able to get through, to say or do something to make him laugh. She'd tell him when it was time to watch TV, and he would listen.

"Sit there," she would say, and for some reason, her command was fine to him. It was like magic.

He knew she was just a little girl, but she was familiar, like the little ones Eva cared for at NPH. They too had bossed him around. It made it easy for him to like her.

Sam and Maggie sat down to watch *Funniest Home Videos*. Tonight, she climbed on the back of the couch with the remote, sitting on his shoulder. The show started, and they were soon laughing loudly. One video showed a dog covered in mud and hiding from his owners. Another featured a baby spitting out vegetables. Next, a cat was falling into a pool, and then a baby could not stop laughing. All of it made them both join in.

Sam liked Maggie, and he loved to laugh. I always marveled at his resilience. Even after all he had been through, humor and laughter still came easy.

I wondered if Maggie reminded him of my girls. They had always loved to laugh with him. How sad they must have been when I died. If I could only see them. I assumed their pain was compounded once Sam was gone too. Did they blame me? Were they angry? How was Rosa, my beautiful Rosa?

On this trip, Maggie was Sam's only bright spot. Juan and Sammy had become more antagonistic as the days passed. When Juan returned from the hospital, he was pushing even more of Sam's buttons. The tension was obvious and growing.

When Juan was released from the hospital, he had a new guitar.

"Where did you get that?" Sam asked.

"From a doctor," Juan said. "He's a resident and was working Sunday morning. It was quiet on the floor, so he sat with me and talked. When he found out I played guitar, he brought two into my room and we played together."

"But how did *you* end up with it?" Sam asked.

"When we finished playing, he gave it to me," Juan said. "He said anyone with talent like me should have their own guitar."

Juan was delighted with his new gift and carried the instrument everywhere. If he did forget it, he would order Sammy to go upstairs and bring it to him.

One evening, Sam was alone upstairs, and Juan's guitar was on the bed. He looked at it like it was his enemy. After a few moments, he walked over to the bed, grabbed the instrument, and raised it up over his head as if he were going to slam it on the floor and break it into pieces. I held my breath, but he stopped short, shaking it with his hands. I could feel his jealousy and his anger. It was uncharacteristic for Sam, but that night, it was palpable.

I wished I could say something, but I was stuck following and observing him from a distance. He couldn't see or hear me. I was still part of his life, yet unable to affect any change in his situation. I even went to school with him, but I couldn't communicate with him. I couldn't help him. I just trailed behind like a shadow.

Marlene had mentioned to Mary Jo that Sam was getting into the habit of sitting around watching Spanish soap operas all day. "It's not good for him. He needs activities," she said.

Never one to shy away from a challenge, Mary Jo researched and found a school where Sam could study English. Soon, he was enrolled at the Romero Center, studying with other students in an ESL (English as a second language) class. These students, both children and adults, had permanently moved to the United States and needed to speak English for school, work, and daily life. Sam, on the other hand, wasn't looking to fit in. He was hoping to leave as soon as possible.

Mel's job was to drive Sam to and from classes, not unlike Sam's job with Father Ron in El Salvador. I liked Mel. He was quiet, not constantly asking questions or needing to talk to Sam.

The two were a good fit. They were comfortable together, driving in silence, listening to the radio, and sometimes commenting on the surroundings. It was how Sam and I traveled together when we were delivering bread. Sam's comfort with Mel made him relax, and eventually, Sam started asking him questions.

"Can I ask something else?" Sam said.

Mel nodded.

"One of my classmates said the teacher 'jumped down her throat.' What does that mean?"

Mel laughed. "English has a lot of slang, just like you have in Spanish, where we use creative ways to explain things. In this case, she meant the teacher got angry and yelled at her."

Sam nodded. After a few moments of silence, Sam spoke again. "English seems so complicated. Like, why are so many words spelled differently but pronounced the same way?"

Mel thought before responding. Unlike Marlene and Mary Jo, he often took a moment to choose his words. "I guess it's because English comes from many languages," he said. "You will find words spelled differently that sound the same and have different meanings. Like 'blue' and 'blew.' One is a color and the other an action."

"Spanish is easier," Sam said, looking out the passenger window.

Mel continued. "There are also words with multiple meanings, like *train*. You can ride on a train, and I can train a dog to do tricks."

"Stupid," Sam grunted, shaking his head. Then they both laughed.

"It's just about learning the vocabulary," Mel said. "It will come, just be patient." They rode the rest of the trip in silence, yet both knew they had made a connection. Ironically, it was words that brought together these two quiet, reflective people.

Sam's heart wasn't into learning English, but like a good soldier, he went to the classes, listened to the teacher, and studied his lessons. The teacher paid special attention to Sam, worrying he might not keep up. Most of the students studied all year long, but Sam came to class only when he and Juan were in Chicago.

As far as I could tell, Sam was a quick study and as good as his fellow students, rapidly catching up on the lessons he missed. He was also learning English from living with the Byrnes and watching TV. His proficiency was obvious when he returned to classes at NPH.

24

Back Again
Sam

OUR TRIPS BECAME ROUTINE. Whether I liked it or not, I was part of the Byrne family. Marlene assigned chores and informed both Juan and me that we needed to pick up our room and clean up after ourselves. She asked us to put dirty clothes in the laundry room by Sunday night. There was to be no food left in our room. She was a bit weary of our visits too.

"Take my clothes down to the laundry," Juan demanded one afternoon.

"No."

"What?" he replied with surprise.

I'd had enough of being his servant, watching everyone fawn over him while he soaked it all in. If he could carry his notebook and guitar up and down the stairs, he could carry his dirty laundry.

"You are only here because of me," he said. "You are supposed to do what I ask."

"You didn't ask," I said. "And I am here to help you when you need it, not be your housemaid."

I kicked the dirty clothes to his side of the room and walked out.

"Get back here!" he yelled as I went downstairs.

"Anything wrong?" Marlene asked as I entered the kitchen.

"No."

She had obviously heard us arguing but she let it go.

Lately, I'd gotten a break from Juan and his antics. Marlene had introduced him to a friend of hers, Nick, a musician and music producer, and they had started playing guitars and singing together.

Marlene had an idea. NPH had a theme song, and she thought it would be nice to have Juan play and record the song and give it to the home so the staff could use it for events and fundraising efforts.

Juan constantly bragged about the recording studio where they practiced. Juan loved the drummer, Christina, and talked about how much she liked his songs. Christina was Nick's sister and had played and toured with numerous bands.

They had been practicing for weeks when Nick came to talk with Brian and Marlene. Juan had shared his own music and Nick offered to record his songs.

I didn't care what they were doing. I was enjoying my alone time at the house; happy they didn't force me to attend every session.

One evening, while Maggie and I were watching TV, Juan returned early, storming through the front door and straight up the stairs to our room. It caught me off guard since Juan was usually in a good mood—and ready to brag—when he returned from a session with Nick.

Marlene stood at the door, talking to Nick. From what I could hear and understand, Nick was talking about Juan's attitude; he was giving everyone a hard time at the studio.

I couldn't help but smirk.

For a week, Juan was irritated and took it out on me. He knew I wouldn't stand up to him in front of Brian and Marlene, so his demands always came in public. "Get me water. Hand me my notebook." He'd leave it upstairs on purpose. I knew exactly what he was doing, but with the tension in the house, I retrieved it without saying a word.

Juan did not discuss the conversation with Brian and Marlene, but it was obvious they had talked to him about his attitude. Five days later, Juan was back at evening practices with Nick and the band, and was far less bossy, even to me.

After a month, Juan's face was sufficiently healed, and we returned home to NPH. My life went back to normal. I loved it. Attending classes. Working in the kitchen. Spending time with Eva. The summer flew by.

In the fall, we were scheduled for another visit to Chicago, and I was excited because his series of surgeries were almost complete. Juan had nose and lip surgery scheduled, and after that, he would get new teeth. The trip was scheduled for eight days. I saw light at the end of the tunnel. Soon it would be over, and we would be home for good.

We arrived in Chicago on a Tuesday at three a.m. The good news was that TACA airlines had a flight from El Salvador that was direct, but the airline could only get a gate at O'Hare in the middle of the night. That was fine with me since a direct flight meant I had to endure only one takeoff and landing.

Juan was incredibly crabby on this trip. He seemed anxious. I didn't ask why, partially because I didn't really care, but also because I didn't want to get him angry. By then, I realized that this experience was extremely difficult, painful, and time-consuming for him. I felt it best to just leave him alone.

Juan would be admitted to Shriners on Thursday and spend the weekend at the hospital recovering. The earlier surgeries on his mouth and nose, and the reconstruction of his face, had already changed his looks dramatically. It was hard to notice while he was recovering, but after the swelling and bruising went down, the change was incredible. He no longer had a wide, flat nose. His lip had a small scar but was connected in the middle. I admit I was happy for him.

We arrived at the hospital early and Juan hopped into his hospital bed. The routine was the same. Crutches in the closet. Legs off and stored. Everyone standing around, waiting.

A nurse arrived for a pre-op check and after taking his temperature, blood pressure, and pulse, she left without a word. It all seemed normal to us.

Doctor Patel came into the room and went straight to Juan. "What is this I am hearing about a fever?" he asked. I could hear the concern in his voice.

"What?" Marlene asked, caught completely by surprise.

"The nurse tells me his temperature is up."

I didn't know what that meant, but Mary Jo and Marlene looked at one another, obviously concerned.

Doctor Patel examined Juan's mouth and explained they would need more tests to check on Juan's progress.

"Why don't you all head to the waiting room, and I'll come in when we have the results," he said.

"What do you think it could be?" Mary Jo asked Marlene as we walked down the long hallway.

"Sam, is there any flu or sickness going around at NPH?" Marlene asked.

"No, I don't think so."

"Did Juan seem sick on the plane?"

"No."

Juan was crabby but I never thought it was because he wasn't feeling well.

We sat quietly waiting for Doctor Patel. When he entered the waiting room, he moved slower than usual. He pulled up a chair and sat down across from Mary Jo and Marlene.

"The last surgery, the one on the roof of his mouth, has not healed as expected, and it's infected," he explained. "Rest assured, the operation was a success, but as we all know, complications sometimes occur, and unfortunately, they don't always present immediately after surgery. The infected tissue will not heal or be strong enough to hold implanted teeth and close the roof of his mouth."

"What does that mean?" Mary Jo asked.

Marlene already had her head down. She knew it was bad.

"The tissue will need to be removed and reconstructed again at a later date once the infection clears up," Doctor Patel said. "Today, I will go in and clean up the palate, removing any damaged tissue. Then, it's a waiting game."

Doctor Patel explained in detail to Marlene and Mary Jo how the medical team would have to use the surgery today to remove the bone graft and start over. He seemed confident that the second try, at a later date, would be successful.

The news was a shock and devastating for everyone. I felt bad for Juan.

"I wanted to tell both of you before I explain everything to Juan," he said as he stood to leave. "We'll make sure he understands everything, and we'll do our best to put his mind at ease."

It was obvious Doctor Patel didn't want us in the room when he talked with Juan.

In tears, Marlene turned to walk down the long hospital hallway. Mary Jo instructed me to stay where I was as she followed Marlene. I knew Mary Jo would help Marlene overcome the disappointment. In fact, Mary Jo saw the bright side of every situation, no matter how troublesome.

After we said our goodbyes to Juan and they wheeled him to surgery, we left the hospital to eat lunch.

Back in the waiting room, it seemed like a long time before Doctor Patel returned. This time his mood was lighter; he walked quickly with a big smile on his face.

"The infection was not as bad as it could have been. We still had to remove the bone graft in the palate, but we were able to perform the first step in the lip and nose reconstruction," he said. "I'm pleased with the outcome and don't think this will set us back too far."

The next time, they would use cadaver tissue instead of cutting more bone from Juan's hip. I thought the idea was repulsive, but he felt the results would be strong. The cadaver tissue would mean an easier recovery, especially for someone who relied on his hips to walk with prosthetics.

Dr. Patel patiently answered Mary Jo's questions before leaving us. "I think this is good news," Mary Jo said. Marlene simply nodded. I could tell she wasn't as optimistic.

When they rolled Juan back into his room from recovery, he looked just as bad as before. Swollen and red, he was letting the nurse try to make him comfortable. There were ice packs propped up against his swollen cheeks and an IV bag hanging over his head.

I felt bad for him and all he was going through. I knew this setback might mean more trips for us, but at that moment, I wasn't thinking about myself. I couldn't imagine facing another round of painful surgery and recovery. Pondering each step of Juan's life, it made sense to me why he would put up a wall to hide his feelings. Why he had such an attitude. And why he always demanded attention from others.

Early the next morning, we entered Juan's hospital room to find he had a roommate. The boy looked to be about 17, Juan's age, and had a swollen face from cleft palate surgery too. Juan was lying back in his bed, television remote in hand, watching a Spanish soap opera.

I settled into the chair to watch while Marlene introduced herself, "Hello, I am Marlene. This is Juan's friend, Samuel."

"Hello, I am Mary, and this is Luke," the woman answered softly.

She wore a blue dress with long sleeves and a full skirt. She had a white bonnet covering her head and wore what looked like an apron around her waist.

Marlene was dressed in a business suit with a jacket and pants. She and I had stopped in for a visit before she went to work.

As the two women chatted, Marlene was trying to explain the strange circumstances of her being the "family member" of two boys from El Salvador. I couldn't help smiling at these two women— and frankly, all of us—who were complete opposites. The woman seemed simple and small, while Marlene seemed tall and strong.

Marlene was telling the woman about Matt and Maggie, and Mary explained she lived in Pennsylvania and had eight children of her own. She was staying at Shriners Family House while Luke had his surgery. The Family House was on the hospital grounds and offered family members a place to live during their child's stay. Like everything else at Shriners, it was free. Mary explained Luke's health issues and how she and her husband decided to allow his cleft palate to be fixed.

"May I ask a favor?" Mary said after we were in the room for a while.

"Of course," Marlene answered.

"They want me to wash Luke's clothing and bedding, but I don't know how," she said.

"There's a laundry room just down the hall," Marlene explained.

"Yes. But I have never used a washing machine," Mary said.

Marlene seemed to understand. "I'll show you," she said and led Mary down the hall holding a bundle of dirty clothes in her arms.

On the drive home, I asked, "Why does that woman dress like that?"

"She belongs to a community called the Amish. They believe in living a simple life," Marlene explained. "They try not to use electricity or buy things from the outside world. Many still travel by horse and buggy and farm with horses. It's a religion and lifestyle that follows a simple existence."

"Why didn't Luke get surgery before now?" I asked.

"I don't know if they typically believe in getting medical care," she explained. "Mary said Luke was suffering from infections and nasal problems from his cleft palate as he got older, so they finally decided to find a way to help him and have him treated at Shriners."

That evening at dinner, Marlene told everyone about Luke and Mary.

"She asked me to help her wash Luke's clothes," Marlene said. "I took her to the laundry room and showed her how to use the washing machine. She wanted to understand how it worked, and I explained both the washer and the dryer to her. She had never used an automatic washer."

"The hospital doesn't do that?" Matthew asked.

"At Shriners, it's the family's responsibility to carry dinner from the cafeteria and wash clothes during recovery," Marlene said. "Many parents live right on the property during their kid's hospital stay."

"How do they wash their clothes at home?" Maggie asked.

"She uses water in a basin and washes everything by hand," Marlene said.

Then, she looked at Brian, smiling, "If I were the mother of eight children, I would march back home and tell you I wanted a washing machine and any other tool or appliance that would make my life easier."

"You wouldn't last a day living a simple existence like Mary does," he said, and they both laughed.

When we arrived at Shriners the next afternoon, Marlene looked up at the television, noticing Juan was again watching a Spanish soap opera. She approached Juan and whispered something in his ear. He changed the station. When I asked her about it later, she said she realized Luke could not use electrical items and was not allowed to touch the remote control. She wanted Juan to change the show to an English channel so that at least Luke could watch and understand what they were saying.

Over the next few days, Mary and Marlene became friends. Juan left the television tuned to English stations and Luke seemed to enjoy the shows. It became clear to me that people who were vastly different could still enjoy one another and share experiences.

25

No More

Sam

"HOLA, PADRE," I SAID as he entered. I had been waiting in his office for what felt like forever. Sitting in a chair with my hands folded in my lap, I kept my head up and stared straight ahead while Father Ron walked around his desk. As he sat down, he calmly folded his hands together on top of a mound of papers before looking up at me.

"What can I do for you, Sam?" he asked.

My fingers squeezed tightly. "I don't want to go back to Chicago."

I had said it. Aloud. Then I looked down. It felt good to finally get it out, but I couldn't look him in the eye.

For months, I had thought about this moment. Dreamed about it. I knew Father Ron and everyone else thought going with Juan was a privilege.

But they didn't know what I knew. They weren't the ones being his caretaker. I hated almost everything. The airplane was scary. The food was different. I had to go to English school with strangers. I missed my friends and my home. And most of all, I missed my time with Eva.

I was sick of being nice to him. Doing whatever he said. But I couldn't tell anyone about that. What would they think of me? I felt guilty just having these feelings. Yet they were real, and I couldn't keep pushing them down. I tried not to think about all the conversations I'd had with other *pequeños* who were jealous of me because I got to go on these trips.

Father Ron sat quietly, tapping his fingers lightly on the stack of papers. Finally, he took a deep breath. I could hear the ticking of the clock on the wall, and just as I was about to continue, he spoke.

"I see. Why?" he asked softly.

"I think, maybe, someone else should get a chance," I said. I hoped he'd think I was being generous, and he wouldn't discover my real feelings.

He didn't seem mad or even surprised. We sat quietly. Tick, tock from the clock.

"So, it's just that you want to give someone else a chance, is that right, Sam?" He didn't wait for a response. "That's very kind of you."

I looked at the floor and nodded. I had to tell a lie.

"Are they good to you while you stay in Chicago, the Byrnes?"

"Yes," I said. "They are nice."

"Are you learning English at Centro Romero? You told me you liked the classes."

"Yes. Camilla, my teacher, is fine," I said. I didn't want to make it about any of these things. It was true—everyone in the United States had been good to me.

"Are you able to help Juan?"

"Yes." I didn't like where this was headed but was prepared to argue my case.

He stood up quickly. "Well, let me think about it. That will be all, Samuel."

Samuel? He never called me Samuel, and when I heard it, my head jerked up, surprised at his response. I had hoped he would tell me his decision. I wanted to stay, plead some more, or wait for him to say okay to my request. But none of that happened. Father Ron just ended the meeting by walking out of his office, leaving me to sit there alone. I looked up, straight into the faces of both

Jesus and Father Wasson in picture frames on the wall behind Father Ron's desk.

On one hand, I felt relief. I had said what I needed to say, and he didn't say no. It meant there was a chance he would agree.

On the other hand, there was a pang in my stomach for being ungrateful. I was jealous of Juan. And jealousy was something Father Ron hated. Many kids would have jumped at this opportunity. They would have been angry if they knew I had asked not to return. I decided to stay quiet and not tell anyone, not even Eva, until Father Ron made his decision.

Time was on Father Ron's side. Everyone had busy schedules, and endless hours of activities, chores, and events to occupy the time until February. Each time he and I caught sight of each other, and he didn't talk to me, my stomach would tie in a knot.

Soon, it was Christmas. Everyone was happy and filled with love during the holiday season. Our celebration at NPH focused on the birth of Christ, but there were also small presents and great food. I was still Father Ron's driver, but he never mentioned our discussion.

On one of our drives, I was able to shop at a small bodega and bought Eva a silver necklace. I could hardly wait to hand her the box and see her face on Christmas morning.

Mass was the first thing we did on Christmas Day. Anticipation for the celebration had everyone excited during the service, from the babies squirming in the arms of the older girls to the boys in the back giggling during the readings. Father Ron began his homily, speaking about rebirth, new beginnings, and hope. He talked about not only opening the wonderful gifts from our friends and family but also accepting God's gifts.

"The meaning of faith is accepting life's gifts from God. The ones we can't unwrap," he said. "Some of these gifts we don't even fully understand. They may show up as opportunities. They may be relationships. So many times, these things have more meaning than the things we can hold or shake. They are not always easy to see, yet they are gifts—great gifts—just the same."

His homily was short, and when he finished, he sat down for reflection. But instead of bowing his head in silent prayer, he looked toward the children in the pews and immediately found me. Sitting next to Eva, I had been feeling happy about being together at Christmas. She was the first to notice Father Ron's stare and looked from him to me and then to him and back at me. When we stood to resume mass, she whispered, "Why was Father staring at you? Are you in trouble?"

I simply shrugged as if I didn't know. The message had come across loud and clear.

Christmas was perfect. Eva loved the necklace. We laughed and danced. It was all so natural.

The week after the holiday, I drove Father Ron to Santa Ana. Christmas decorations still dotted the streets and neighborhoods. A nativity scene was on display in front of one of the churches.

"Sam, what do you think Jesus means at Christmas?" he asked after riding in silence for some time.

"He is our savior," I replied.

"Yes," he said. "But he was a gift, perhaps the best gift of all."

I was quiet. What was I supposed to say? A few miles later, Father Ron continued.

"Sometimes, I wonder about when Mary found out she was pregnant. What was her first thought? Was she scared? Do you think she was unsure about accepting what would become an incredible gift from God? Was she angry to be the one chosen to carry the burden? I mean, how did she really feel at that moment?"

I stared straight ahead, gripping the steering wheel and keeping my eyes glued to the road. (After our accident, some time ago, I rarely broke focus on the road ahead of me.)

A few more minutes of silence. And then, he continued. "Life is like that," he said. "We get opportunities, but sometimes we don't realize right away what gifts they are."

I was trying to think of something to say but he didn't give me a chance.

"Sam, your opportunity in Chicago, and with Juan, is a gift. It might not seem like it now, but I promise someday it will, sooner than you think."

We were both quiet for a moment. He really wanted me to think about what he was saying, and the silences were intentional, to let his words sink in. "I want you to accept what God has offered with this opportunity. I want you to see it as a gift. I believe in my heart it will become invaluable in the future. Maybe it will be the best gift of all."

There was no sense arguing, so I simply nodded. I would have to keep going to Chicago, to see it through, not because I agreed with the decision, but out of respect.

"And, Sam, I have one more request," he said. "When you go back to Chicago, embrace the opportunity you have in front of you. Keep studying English. Be part of the Byrne family. Engage with them. And open your heart to Juan. I know that might be hard, but please do your best. Enjoy this time because it will be over quickly."

"Yes, Father," I replied, stopping to let the pedestrians cross the road. It was then he looked at me and smiled.

"Put your heart into the opportunity, and I promise you'll receive gifts you never imagined."

26

Music Practice

Sam

"THAT'S NOT RIGHT." Nick wasn't yelling, but he was mad. Christina, the drummer and Nick's sister, stopped playing and looked at him.

"What's wrong with it?" she yelled back across the studio.

"You're off the beat. Just listen," he said. Then he played the song back to her on the guitar.

"That's what I did," she said. Now, she was getting mad.

"No, it's not," Nick said. "This must be right! Now, listen again!"

Juan liked it when Christina and Nick argued. At first, I thought it was because when they fought, Nick wasn't yelling at him. But he liked it when Christina stood up to Nick. Juan didn't argue with Nick anymore because he wanted to play his music. Brian had set him straight, telling him if he wanted Nick to collaborate with him, he'd have to change his attitude. That's why he liked when Christina did it. It gave him the "fix" that he needed; to see someone stand up to Nick.

Christina threw down her drumsticks, stood up, ripped off her sweatshirt, threw it on the floor, and then sat down again. She was Nick's sister, so they could fight like this, like family. She was also an amazing drummer so Nick let her get away with things.

"Fine! Let's go again," she said, half smiling, half serious.

I loved watching her play. I had never seen anything like it. Her beautiful, long hair flew as she slammed her sticks. In the NPH music troupe, each musician played just one drum. Christina sat behind a full set of drums and cymbals. Encircling her, she looked small, but when she played, she was powerful and moved so fast you couldn't tell which drum she was hitting.

The musicians started to play again, and within a few seconds, Nick yelled, "That's it! You've got it!"

Maggie had let me borrow her Nintendo DS for something to do at the studio while the band practiced, but instead, I sat watching. Juan had been going to the studio for weeks. Marlene and Nick decided that Juan would record the NPH song, along with a CD of his own music. They had even planned for Juan to perform at a concert. Nick would produce the show and was demanding perfection from all the musicians, including Juan.

Finally, they finished recording the last song and everyone celebrated. I was happy to be finished with the endless nights in the studio. I didn't always go along, but lately, I felt obligated to participate in case Juan needed me.

Remembering my argument with Juan and my talk outside the NPH dining hall with Eva, I was trying to be nicer. It was easier since we had only one more visit before the entire thing would be over. I started helping more and easing up on Juan. He was having trouble learning to walk with his new legs, so it was natural for me to take on some extra duties to ease the burden for him.

Nick went to a little refrigerator beside the couch in the recording booth and pulled out a bottle of champagne.

"Come on, Sam, you're celebrating too," he said as he walked from the booth to the studio.

I threw the Nintendo into the backpack, right next to Juan's green notebook, and followed. Nick ripped the shiny paper off the top of the bottle and pushed on the edge of the cork. I ducked behind a speaker.

"Sam, are you scared of a little cork?" Nick said, laughing.

"Won't it spray all over?" I asked. I'd seen people open bottles like that in movies.

"Only if you shake it. And we want to drink it!" he said as the cork popped. Nick poured equal amounts into small plastic cups lined up on a table.

The musicians were stowing their equipment and Juan was sitting on a stool in the middle of the room. Nick handed him the first glass.

"Well, Juan you did it," he said, touching his cup to Juan's. "It's a big deal finishing ten songs and recording the tracks. How do you feel?"

Juan was smiling. It was the happiest I had ever seen him.

"Good, very good," he replied.

"There's still one really big, unfinished job," Nick said.

Juan looked puzzled.

"What do we call it?" Nick asked. "Every great album needs a great name."

"I don't know," Juan replied.

"Well, you have talked about doing the concert for Haiti, and I think helping people affected by the earthquake—especially those who lost limbs—is a fantastic idea. Does that inspire any ideas?"

On January 12, 2010, Olegario received word that a devastating earthquake had hit Haiti. NPH had a home there and we awaited information on the damage. We considered all the children of NPH our family. Father Ron said Mass for everyone struggling in a country with limited resources and so much tragedy. He again talked about "simple" gifts such as health, water, and safety. We all prayed for our "brothers and sisters" at NPH Haiti and for the staff trying to care for them during such a terrible natural disaster.

I hadn't realized Juan wanted to dedicate his concert to the amputees suffering from the Haiti earthquake. It made me look at him differently. Eva was right when she said he was not a bad person. Was *I* the selfish one?

Juan thought about it for a moment, then nodded his head.

"What about you, Sam? Do you have any ideas?" Nick asked as he handed me a cup of champagne. I took a drink, it was sweet and bubbly, making my nose tingle.

"No," I answered. I had never tasted champagne, so I was savoring my first sip. Besides, this was Juan's thing, not mine.

"How about NPH? Does that give you any inspiration? You both talk about Father Wasson," Nick said as he passed out champagne to the other musicians sitting in a circle around Juan.

"Tell the guys about NPH," Christina said. Juan smiled as she talked. He was almost giddy when she gave him attention.

Juan told the band the story of Father Wasson, and how he started NPH by saving a young boy arrested for stealing the collection money from his church in Mexico. Father Wasson convinced the judge not to sentence the boy to jail time, and he became the first *pequeño* at NPH. Now there were homes in nine countries.

"We are all grateful for Father Wasson," I said after Juan told the story, looking at him with a smile. I had to admit, I loved the idea of giving Father Wasson credit on the CD. He had saved us all.

For the next twenty minutes, Nick and the band brainstormed names for the album. I sat quietly, sipping on my champagne. I liked it. After I finished my cup, Nick poured me another. The ideas were crazy, but the banter was fun.

"Central Music."

"Standing Up for NPH."

"How about 'Sound in the Central'?"

"Stand On New Legs?"

"Music Has Legs?" Everyone laughed at that one, even Juan.

"Well, we do need a name," Nick finally said. "Go home and think about it."

"What about gratitude?" Juan asked.

"What about it?" Nick replied.

"Maybe the title needs to say thank you," Juan said.

Everyone around the room nodded. Nick looked surprised. "That's a great theme," he said. I could see he was happy. It was the first time I realized Nick and Juan had become friends.

"The Sound of Gratitude," Christina chimed in.

One of the band members repeated it in Spanish, "*Sonido de Gratitud.*"

The room was silent, and then, Juan smiled. He nodded and repeated it in Spanish. That was it: *Sonido de Gratitud.*

The week before the concert, a reporter came to the house to interview Juan. They were amazed at his story and, at that moment, so was I. Even though I could have recited every word, it was as if I were hearing it for the first time. Born with a cleft palate. Burned as a child. Both legs amputated. Living on the streets. Coming to NPH. Having all those surgeries. And now, he'd be performing on the stage at the Park West in Chicago. A real musician.

After the reporter left, Juan came into the bedroom. I was lying on my little bed on the floor. I didn't say anything as he hopped up onto his bed and turned out the light.

"I hope I can perform," he almost whispered. "I'm scared."

"I know," I said, matching his whisper.

I should have said more but I didn't. He was nervous, and I knew he would never tell anyone else. As I lay there in the dark, I started thinking. *What if he* can't *perform? Should I tell Marlene? Or talk to Father Ron?*

The whole night I felt horrible, tossing, turning, and thinking. I realized just how jealous of Juan I had been.

At once, I decided to stop. I would give up trying to compete. I was lucky. Eva and Father Ron reminded me of all the positives in my own life. I had my legs. I wasn't the one who had to endure surgery after surgery. I could hear Eva saying, "Make something of yourself rather than wanting what someone else has." I needed to be happy for him. More importantly, I needed to be happy for myself.

For the next week, Juan was quiet. I noticed he would take his guitar with him everywhere but didn't play it. He went to practice but said nothing when he came home. I saw him reading the lyrics in his green notebook over and over. I wondered if he was forgetting the words to his songs and needed to remind himself. His statement kept going through my head, *I hope I can perform. I'm scared.*

On the Thursday before the concert, he came to bed late. He had been at the final practice with Nick, and after, they had gone to the theater to stand on the stage where they would perform.

I waited for Juan to turn on the lights. But tonight, he walked straight into the bathroom and shut the door. He was there for a long time. I listened but didn't hear any movement or sound.

When the door finally opened, I could see his shadow. He had taken off his legs and was hopping up on his bed in the dark. I waited for a minute.

"Juan?"

"Yes?"

"I know you are scared. This is big," I said. He didn't say anything. "Just remember, you are a good musician. Your songs are great, people love you, and the musicians playing with you have your back. I've watched you from the beginning, at practice, at NPH, and even here in the house. More than anyone, *I* know you can do this."

He was silent.

"When you see them, the audience, just pretend you are home at NPH playing for the kids, the ones you sing to every Saturday night at Mass And at Christmas. Then, it won't be scary."

The room was quiet for a moment.

"Thank you," he said quietly.

I rolled over, feeling better about myself and Juan.

27

The Concert
Jorge

"WHERE'S JUAN?" SAM ASKED casually, but on the inside, I knew he was anxious. The days leading up to this event had been chaotic. Juan was quiet, to say the least. Maybe angry. Maybe scared. I wasn't sure. Nick was juggling musicians, equipment, and rehearsals. Even Marlene was yelling at the kids. Everyone was on edge.

I had never seen anything like it. The stage. The lights. All the equipment. Back home in El Salvador, street musicians were common, but it was unusual to have a guitar or an instrument. Most of the time, they were banging on buckets or singing a cappella.

Everyone was amazed by the turnout. Tickets sold quickly. Friends and family were there. Groups, like the staff of Shriners and the El Salvadoran Consulate, had stepped up in a big way. Musicians volunteered their time. Nick had been right about Juan's story; it was like a snowball. The media picked up on the press release and Juan's story was covered on radio, TV, and in newspapers. His front-page story in *The Chicago Tribune* incited the most interest. People wanted to see the rock stars who had volunteered to sing at the charity concert, but they also wanted to know more about Juan Manuel.

On the street in front of the Park West Theater, TV station trucks lined the curb, including one from the Spanish station. I recognized the call letters from the soap opera the boys watched.

Sam walked around the theater, took the side stairs up to the stage, and then explored behind the curtain. He was looking for Juan but also enjoying the freedom of being a VIP at the event.

Everyone was looking for Juan. Danielle, Nick's wife, asked Sam to keep an eye out for him. Sam was canvasing the venue but kept being recognized by attendees. Stopping to greet and thank everyone, he kept a constant eye for any sign of Juan. Where had he gone?

Sam entered the green room at the back of the theater, which was bustling with energy. Steve Augeri (the lead singer for Journey after Steve Perry left the band) had arrived, and everyone was clamoring to meet him. Nick had connections and was able to get him to agree to perform as part of the concert. Christina introduced Sam to Steve. Before the concert, Marlene explained that he was part of one of the most popular bands in the US. Sam had never heard of Journey but had become a fan by listening to the songs.

Sam continued down the hallway and returned backstage where Nick was examining the final setup.

"How's it going?" Sam asked.

Nick was sweating and still in his "work" clothes, putting the finishing touches on the stage with the crew. "We're almost set."

Nick's intensity was obvious, and it made Sam even more panicked.

"Have you seen Juan?" Sam asked nonchalantly.

"Nope, not back here," Nick replied as he moved another piece of gear.

Juan had been nervous all week. Sam hoped to give him a pep talk and allow him a quiet moment to collect himself before going on stage.

Sam went to the other side of the theater and down the back stairs to the dock where the bands unloaded equipment. The sides of the hallway were lined with wooden crates, and it was dark. On the left, a light shone from a small room. Sam found Juan standing with Father Ron, who had flown in for the event. Father Ron's hand was on Juan's shoulder and both of their heads were bowed, praying together.

The scene was peaceful. Sam stood and watched in silence. I could feel him relax.

When they finished, Juan looked up at Sam and they both smiled. Father Ron noticed the connection and smiled too.

"There are a few more reporters who want to speak with us," Sam said.

For the next thirty minutes, Juan and Sam answered questions, repeating the story about Juan's journey, NPH, the surgeries at Shriners, and the music. Juan was looking around; he was desperately searching for something.

The boys returned backstage, and Juan peeked through the curtains. The seats were filling up with so many faces he recognized. The doctors and nurses from Shriners were in the front row. The NPH staff from the Chicago office were off to the left. Friends, neighbors, and people from the parish were getting seated. The teachers from the Romero Center and the staff from the Chicago Consulate of El Salvador were sitting dead center.

Juan turned his body to face Sam.

"Thank you. I am glad you are here with me, not just tonight, but for the whole time," Juan said. "I don't think I could have done this without you."

"You will be great," Sam said, smiling. "I know you can do this. Just keep saying it over and over. Say 'I can do this' out loud. It works."

Juan nodded and gave Sam a genuine, grateful smile. They shook hands. Then, Sam put his hand on Juan's shoulder and pulled him into an embrace.

Nick appeared on the other side of the stage, now in his performance outfit, black pants and a button-down shirt with rhinestones. It was time.

Juan started walking onto the stage.

"No, Juan," Nick motioned from the wings across the stage, pointing to where Juan was supposed to wait and enter after Nick introduced him. They had talked about this, even rehearsed it. It didn't matter. Juan just kept walking onto the stage, and Nick, realizing he couldn't stop Juan, did the same.

When Juan reached Nick, he put a hand on his shoulder and they embraced. I could see Nick smile as Juan returned to his spot in the wings.

Marlene started the show by thanking everyone, and the curtains opened to a huge screen. A video began to play, telling the story of NPH's homes in nine countries. It explained the tremendous tragedy in Haiti after the 2010 earthquake; how the hospital was caring for victims. How amputations, just like Juan's, were a major part of keeping people, who had been trapped in the rubble, alive. Juan was on screen explaining he wanted the proceeds from the concert to help others like him: innocent amputees whose lives changed due to tragedies they could not predict or control. He wanted them to receive prosthetics and walk again.

The audience took it all in. The tone was somber and respectful. The room went quiet.

After the video, Nick and the band played a warm-up song to start the night. He wanted to bring them back to the fun of the evening before introducing Juan.

Just as Nick planned, the audience was fired up before Juan even took the stage. Nick knew the value of building suspense, excitement, and expectation, and with each passing moment, that's exactly what was happening.

Nick had explained to the band weeks prior, "Juan doesn't have that many songs, so we need to craft a concert that both introduces him and entertains."

I could see Juan nervous in the wings across the stage. Waiting.

"And now, I give you the man of the hour, Juan Manuel Pineda!"

Nick introduced Juan as though he was a top-tier rock star. A member of the crew put a stool down center stage as Juan walked out using crutches and his new legs.

He sat down to a standing ovation. He didn't smile. He set his crutches down on the floor next to him and adjusted his prosthetic legs, moving each with his hands. As he put the guitar strap around his shoulder, he looked down at the floor. Again, the room fell quiet. About the time everyone was getting uncomfortable with the silence, Juan looked at Nick. Juan's fingers started flying over the guitar, softly at first as the band chimed in. He was sitting up tall. His voice was perfect. He smiled the beautiful smile given to him by the doctors. He was as happy as I had ever seen him. A performer. A man.

The audience was spellbound.

The first song ended, and the crowd went wild. When things quieted, Juan sat perfectly still, stoically looking down at his guitar. The musicians were waiting for his signal to start the second song. But this time, they appeared much more confident in following his lead.

He leaned into the microphone. "I want to say *gracias* to all of you. It is not always easy, this surgery, this music," he said, looking back at Nick. "But I love you all more than you will ever know. I also want to thank my friend Sam and NPH who helped me to get here."

Then he smiled, strummed his guitar and the music started again. He was a success, and Sam's work was done.

28

Come Again?
Sam

THIS TIME, I HARDLY noticed the plane taking off. It should have been because I was happy. I was finished going to Chicago and finally on my way back to Eva. What more could I want?

But it wasn't happiness that had me too preoccupied to focus on the movement of the plane. It was something Brian and Marlene told me before we left for the airport.

I was sitting at the kitchen counter when they sat down on either side of me. Marlene looked excited. Immediately, I started to worry. Marlene said Camilla, my teacher at the Romero Center, told her I was the best student. I smiled and felt relieved. It was a nice complement, something I'd cherish.

But Marlene continued. "She said you're learning English faster than most of the full-time students, and she thinks you should go to college here, in the US."

I was stunned. It was a nice offer, and I'm sure a wonderful opportunity that others in my situation would jump at.

Brian and Marlene said they would support me and pay for college if I wanted to go.

I didn't know how to respond. They'd all been so generous. In my panic, I simply said thank you and that I'd think about it. But the truth was, I didn't want to come back. I wanted to go home.

As the plane raced down the runway for takeoff, I felt conflicted. For weeks, I couldn't wait to get home and never go back to the United States. Now, there was a pang in my stomach—and sadness—when I started to think about how much I'd miss everyone. I never thought I would feel sad about leaving Chicago. It was a surprise. The emotions flooded in. How long would they last? Days? Weeks? Forever?

Even on the ride to the airport, I felt emotion bubbling up, but I tried to push it down, drowning it out with thoughts of Eva and NPH.

I hugged Murphy. I shoved my face into his fur, remembering how afraid of him I had been that first night. He had become my friend and companion. As if he knew, his big body leaned in and fell into my lap. Did he understand? Would I ever see him again?

Maggie was crying, hiding her face in Marlene's hip. "Why do you have to leave?" she asked.

Matt shook my hand.

On the other hand, Juan seemed fine. He had copies of his CD and was taking his new guitar with him on the plane. I noticed he packed the green notebook in his checked luggage this time.

Before we left for the airport, Marlene made a final attempt. "We talked with Father Ron about this opportunity, Sam, but you don't have to make a decision now," she said, easing my anxiety. "We would help you apply for a student visa and other paperwork if you wanted to attend school. Just let us know your decision."

It might have been easier if I had said no right then and there, but I couldn't do it. I would have to face Father Ron back in El Salvador and pretend to think it over before declining.

The trip home seemed to last forever. Juan and I barely spoke. Like at the end of any big event—the day after Christmas, the morning after a wedding—there is an emotional letdown. We were both feeling it.

Eva was there when we arrived, which quickly changed my mood. She couldn't wait to hear about the concert and made me tell her every detail of the story from start to finish.

"What else happened?" she kept asking.

We were sitting together under a tree and finally, I ran out of things to say.

"No, there's nothing else," I said, realizing how exhausted I was from the travel and the stress of considering the offer.

"Really? Nothing else?" she asked, crossing her arms.

I had no idea what she was talking about.

"Like perhaps being given the opportunity to go to college in the United States?"

I was shocked. All I could say was, "How?"

"Father Ron told me the Byrnes offered to pay for you to go to college in Chicago. Aren't you excited?" she asked. Clearly, she thought this was a good idea.

"No," I replied. "I am not going to leave and study there."

"Yes, you are," she said.

"No, I am not."

We were called away for dinner, but I knew the conversation was not over. Father Ron had counted on the fact that she would try to convince me. He knew she was his best chance at changing my mind. He was good.

The next day, Eva brought it up again, but with a gentler approach.

"Sam, we are all going to leave here someday," she said, touching my hand. "Next year, everyone our age will be living at the boys' and girls' college houses," she said. "Just imagine how a college degree from the U.S. will help your future ... *our* future. We've talked about building a family and supporting ourselves. I think it would be a wonderful way to do it."

"I just don't want to leave. It's too far away," I argued.

"But we'll be far away from each other at the college houses too," she said. "We won't see each other."

Our discussions continued for a week before Father Ron called me to his office. Olegario was there as well, and they acted like it was new to all of us, like they were telling me about it for the first time. It was all I had been thinking about for days.

"Sam, you can try it, and if you don't like it, you can return to college here," Olegario promised. "Being bilingual will be a huge advantage when you want to get a job."

I was the only one who didn't see this as a great opportunity. Why would I want to leave my country? It was too far away. I knew I didn't want to leave Eva. What if I couldn't get good grades? What if something happened while I was away?

I would have to convince them I should stay here.

29

Airport Goodbye
Jorge

THERE WE WERE AGAIN. Waiting at the airport. As I watched Sam sitting at the gate, I could feel his sadness. He was already homesick. I sat next to him, but of course, he didn't know I was there. I could have reached out and touched him, but of course, he wouldn't feel it.

I had been there, right next to him, for it all: Father Ron talking to him about studying in the US. Eva encouraging him to take the opportunity. Olegario almost forcing him to go because he knew what a wonderful chance it was; one that few *pequeños* would ever get. It also meant one less child to educate, feed, and clothe. I understood the pressure.

Sam didn't want to go, but the people he loved and respected most in the world had convinced him he should. If I had been there in body, I would have pushed him too. It was his chance at a better future. But at that time, he just didn't see it.

It wasn't that he didn't like the Byrne family, but he missed his culture, NPH, and of course, Eva. She argued for days, telling him to go because they would both be in college for the next few years anyway. What doors would this education open for them? A degree from a United States university might take them far. They often talked about their future. About being together. Having a family. She had argued that none of that could happen until she became a nurse and he got his education.

So, there he was, waiting to get on a plane back to Chicago, and this time, it was different. This time, he wasn't doing it for Juan. But he wasn't doing it for himself either. Once again, Sam was making others happy.

Something felt different for me as well. Something was changing. Things were slowing down. It was almost like the feeling you get when you might faint.

As he walked to get in line at the gate, I realized I could not move. I didn't understand what was happening. I was frozen, standing at the back of the crowd, watching as they scanned his boarding pass.

I hadn't had any control since my death, and I didn't have control here. I just knew I would not be going with Sam.

He handed the attendant his papers, but instead of following the other passengers down the jetway, he stopped and glanced back. It was like he was looking for me. I didn't understand. Could he suddenly see me? I waved but there was no reaction. Then, he turned, walked through the door and was gone.

This time, Sam was going alone.

30

Airport Goodbye
Sam

LEAVING THROUGH THE GATES of NPH seemed to happen in slow motion. Eva snuck out of her dorm so we could say our final goodbyes. We held each other in a tight embrace before I slid into the passenger seat of the car. Luis was driving, and as we rolled out of the gate, my entire body twisted around to stare back at her. She was standing on the grass, smiling, and waving. I was sure Eva would cry but she never did. I watched out the back window as she got smaller and further away until she was gone. My stomach had a sick feeling that radiated throughout my whole body. Homesickness was already setting in. A tear rolled down my cheek. I wiped it away, staring down at my wet fingers.

Luis pulled up to the airport and simply said goodbye. Without another word, I was left standing on the curb watching the car merge into traffic.

Like a zombie, I made my way through the airport and to the waiting area at my gate and just sat there. For the first time, I wished Juan were with me. I needed someone, a friend, to get through this.

The agent announced: "Passengers in boarding group four can enter through gate 27."

I was in line with my boarding pass and passport. My ticket said, "one way," and it made my stomach drop to read it.

Something made me turn around. It was as if I heard someone call my name or recognized a familiar face in the crowd. A last look, perhaps? No, it was something bigger, a sign. As I turned back to face the gate agent, I swear I saw *him*. He was there. It was Jorge, standing in a white shirt in the back of the waiting area. He was smiling and waving at me, looking just like he did the last day we were together delivering bread. The agent scanned my boarding pass and was trying to hand it back. She looked at me, puzzled that I was holding up the line.

"Are you waiting for someone?" the attendant asked.

"No."

"Then you can move along, sir, you are good to go," she said.

I craned my neck as I started to walk. I must be seeing things. I had been dropped off alone. No one was here. Certainly not Jorge.

I shook my head and walked through the door.

31

English Academy
Sam

I **NEVER THOUGHT** I could miss Juan Manuel, but sitting in seat 22A staring at the clouds, I wanted him next to me. For one thing, he would have taken the window seat and blocked my view outside. It would have made it easier to stare at the back of the seat in front of me and try to forget I was miles off the ground. Even though I wanted to ignore it, I could see outside in my peripheral vision as the plane rocked. First, the ground passed by, then the blue sky turned again to a green landscape as the plane tilted. As we ascended, clouds began rushing past the wing.

Alone. I should be used to it. The isolation. That feeling of disconnection while surrounded by people. The man next to me was sleeping. On the aisle, a woman looked relaxed as she read a book.

I replayed the discussion with Father Ron and Olegario in my head. "This is an amazing opportunity. You should be so proud of your accomplishments."

The Byrnes had talked to Father Ron and offered me the chance to attend college in Chicago. I would continue my English studies at the DePaul English Language Academy with students from all over the world. Father Ron explained how I would work to become fluent and then take a college entrance exam called the TOEFL, which stands for Test of English as a Foreign Language.

The whole time they were explaining the plan, I was conjuring up a list of excuses why I shouldn't go.

"I don't want you to answer now," Father Ron had said. He knew I needed time to go away and think about the opportunity.

In the end, I agreed to go. Eva was the one to finally convince me. We agreed that we would both graduate and then build our life together.

I wish time could stand still; that when life was good, you could keep everything just as it is. Take my time at NPH with Eva, for example. There were so few times I was genuinely happy, and it always seemed fleeting.

What would Jorge think if he saw me now?

What would the guys from the streets—especially Jefe and Loba—think? I often thought about how I had been spared prosecution for our crimes because of my age. I imagined Jefe in the detention center, a jail for teenagers. In my mind, he lived in a small, cold, barracks-style room. The food would be worse than at the orphanage, and the boys there were certainly meaner. No one I asked could confirm his location or if he'd been released. Even Jose had lost contact with all of them.

I knew I didn't want to choose a life that might include detention or jail, a terrible existence. Jorge had warned me repeatedly to avoid anything criminal so I wouldn't end up in an El Salvador jail. He painted a bleak picture of life on the inside.

During our discussion, Father Ron reminded me of how lucky I had been in my life. The road seemed to turn right for me at the most desperate times. Was this another right turn?

I knew they would be waiting at the bottom of the escalator, standing together. It felt the same but so different. When Juan and I traveled, we had to be the last passengers off the plane and take the elevator with his wheelchair attendant. This time, I was in a herd of people from my flight riding down the escalator headed for baggage claim.

Brian, Marlene, Mel, and Mary Jo had all come to greet me, and we waited together for my luggage to arrive on the conveyor belt. It felt good to see familiar faces in the bustle of the airport, and I was excited to see Murphy again. It had been five months since Juan's final trip and the concert.

When my large suitcase appeared on the baggage belt, I was relieved that my belongings had not been lost. Father Ron had instructed me to pack more clothes than I thought I needed, to get long pants, and take along an extra pair or two of shoes. It felt strange taking so many things from the folded piles at NPH and packing a huge suitcase.

The car ride "home" was animated as Mary Jo and Marlene asked questions and talked about school. They were thrilled that I was going to start at DePaul.

I lugged the big suitcase from the car into the house. It was missing a wheel and no longer rolled. So as not to let them notice, I carried it even though it was heavy. All the suitcases at NPH were old. We would get supplies for the orphanage when guests visited. People would fill old suitcases with toothbrushes, diapers, or other supplies and take them to NPH. They left the empty suitcases behind, and they were stacked in the warehouse in piles when I went to find this one.

Murphy was at the door when we arrived. At first, he was barking, but once he saw me, his tail went crazy. I started scratching his back and dropped to the floor as he tried to climb into my lap. It was natural and comforting to bury my face in his fur and scratch away.

Step by step, I dragged the suitcase upstairs. The twin mattress—my old bed—was no longer on the floor and I realized the big bed was mine. I plopped down on the soft comforter and stretched out. This was the first time I'd ever had a room to myself. It seemed odd to be in a bed this big. For a moment, I was happy. But as I looked around and realized Juan would not be there, loneliness took over. There was solace in having someone nearby, whether it was Juan in this room or my street friends under a bridge.

I was staring at the ceiling when Murphy jumped up on the mattress. He had followed me upstairs but I hadn't noticed. He moved quietly for a big dog but there was no denying his presence as he settled in next to me, curling up and leaning on my hip. I rested my arm on his back and started petting him. He made me calm and happy.

On my first day of school, Mel rode the L train with me to downtown Chicago. He would meet me after class and planned to ride back and forth from the neighborhood all week. It was a short walk from Mel and Mary Jo's to the Byrnes. Mel had commuted to work on the train his entire career and wanted me to understand the L system before I rode it alone.

Mel was patient and explained everything, from the turnstiles to the platforms and the signage at the stops. The CTA Ventra card was confusing. He bought me the first card and explained that it could be reloaded when I needed more money for fares. How would I know when to refill? I was afraid of getting to the station, swiping my card, and not being able to unlock the turnstile.

The Blue Line platform was close to DePaul's campus, and it was a short walk to my building. On the L, Mel sat quietly. I loved his stable presence and the fact we didn't always have to talk.

"I'll meet you here after class," he said at the door. I nodded as I turned to make my way to class.

The English Language Academy took up three consecutive floors of a high-rise building. Moving from class to class would be easy. The previous week, Marlene and I took a tour during orientation, and that helped ease any anxiety the first few days.

The director, Anders, was a tall blond man from Sweden who startled me with the strength of his handshake.

"Sammy!" he yelled from his office door as I exited the elevator.

Anders had an office off the main floor and made a point to hang around the lounge and engage with the students between classes.

"So great to have you here. I want to introduce you to another new DePaul student," he said.

A tall, skinny Chinese boy stood in the lobby wearing an "I ♥ NY" T-shirt and a pair of white Converse high-tops. He extended his hand with a huge smile on his face. Anders explained that we were both starting the program with similar English proficiency and would be on the same class track.

"The two of you should get to know each other and practice speaking in English together," Anders said.

"I am Lántiān, but you can call me Blue Sky, which is how it translates to English," he said. "The Chinese pronunciation is too hard."

"I am Samuel," I replied. "But I go by Sam or Sammy."

"I like Sammy," he smiled.

Blue Sky started talking about what he liked in America, which was everything.

"Do you like Chipotle?" he asked and then continued without waiting for an answer. "I love all American food—coffee, donuts, street tacos—it's all great."

The lounge was clearing out and we walked together to our first class. Blue Sky compared our schedules; they were identical. Our English wasn't perfect, but we were both more proficient than many of the foreign students in the program. Some students arrived without knowing any vocabulary at all.

Over the next few weeks, Blue Sky and I became inseparable. He was so excited about being in America to study that it was contagious. Every day, we went to a different restaurant for lunch; hamburgers, tacos, Indian food—we tried them all. The only thing he did not want to eat was American Chinese food. Most afternoons, I could hardly concentrate because I was so full. I had a habit of eating too much, still expecting I might be hungry in the future. He ate too much just because he loved food. It was amazing he stayed so skinny.

Perhaps it was our immense differences from everyone else or the single commonality of our studies, but Blue Sky felt more familiar to me than anyone in the US. We could make stupid mistakes as we tried to navigate the city with a map or struggle to say the right thing when we ordered food without judgment from the other. Laughing at ourselves became natural and infectious.

"Today, we must try Buffalo Wild Wings," Blue Sky announced as we sat down in our morning class.

I didn't have time to ask what that was or argue that I wasn't sure I wanted to eat buffalo because, at that moment, the teacher entered and began giving the class instructions.

At lunchtime, Blue Sky laughed all the way to the restaurant after I asked him about the food. We walked blocks and blocks, turning left and then right as his phone directed us. I felt like we were walking in circles.

Finally, we arrived and found a table among the crowd. He ordered a basket of wings. They looked like chicken to me and tasted great. I was throwing the bones in a basket when I noticed Blue Sky crunching away.

"What are you doing?" I asked.

"What?" He looked at me with wing sauce all over his hands and face.

"Are you eating the bones?"

"They're great," he said and kept right on chomping. "Try it."

"No way."

I could not stop laughing. People around us at the restaurant noticed and were laughing too. Blue Sky didn't care.

Blue Sky's dream was to work in animation for the movie industry. He planned to become proficient in English and move to California, specifically Hollywood, to study and work in the movie business.

"I want to be a great animator," he said. "What is your dream, Sam?"

"I don't know." I had never considered having a dream; I focused on survival. The opportunities I had were either given or ordered. Nothing had been my own choice.

"What do you mean? You must have a dream for the future," he continued.

"The only thing I ever considered was being with Eva," I said.

Over the past few weeks, I had told him my life story. He would listen intently, then shake his head in disbelief. "You must have a lucky charm to be rescued so many times," he said one day at lunch.

Today, he was more serious.

"You were given this chance to build a life, any life you want. You must dream big," he said.

I thought about it for a minute while he continued to ramble. "What do you want to do? Is there something you are passionate about? Where do you want to live?"

His questions ran through my head as I stared out the window of the train on my way home. All those houses and apartments along the route to downtown Chicago were filled with people who had dreams and were building lives. Did they all know the answers? Did they all have a dream?

I could not visualize anything in the future except Eva. She was the one thing I knew I wanted. Would we be married? I could see her working as a nurse, just as she planned. I would have a job but could not visualize what it would be. Not a doctor. Nothing in medicine. Maybe I would manage an NPH home like Olegario. Maybe I could do computer work. The idea of planning for a future beyond finding food for the day or getting my hands on money seemed silly. Did dreaming help find happiness?

Blue Sky didn't ask me about my plans again for a few months. By summer, we had both advanced in our coursework. We were learning grammar and writing, and the classes were more challenging.

I invited Blue Sky to the Byrnes' lake house for a weekend in early July. He'd been to their house for dinner several times and everyone got along. It was hard not to like Blue Sky. He was always laughing, and he loved to talk about anything.

He told us about his family and growing up in China, but his curiosity about everything American and facts about the way people lived usually sidetracked him. He wanted to know about Marlene's company. Why had Brian become a police officer? What criminals did he arrest? Did he ever meet a gangster? He even asked the kids about their school, which created conversation far beyond anything I had ever discussed with them. He was fascinated by everything, and without question, was the most curious person I had ever met.

At the lake, it was no different. He asked questions about the pontoon boat as we rode on the lake. He also had questions about the lake. "Is that a public beach? What fish are in the lake? How deep is the water?"

He loved jumping into the middle of the lake after we anchored. Marlene, always cautious when it came to water, asked us to wear life jackets. After Blue Sky convinced Marlene to let him jump in one more time, we both put them on and floated in the water.

Lily Lake is a small lake in Wisconsin, and the Byrnes owned property with four small cottages. Brian's brother and his family had the house next door. On this weekend, both families were at the lake, which meant Matt and Maggie's three cousins, two dogs, and two more adults were there. With Blue Sky and me along, it made for a large group. We played games, swam, and had a bonfire in the evening. Blue Sky soaked it all in.

On the second morning, I woke up to Brian shaking my shoulder. "Sam, Blue Sky has taken a kayak to the center of the lake. We better ride out on the boat and make sure he's okay."

As we walked down to the shore, I saw Blue Sky sitting in a kayak in the center of the calm, morning lake. It was quiet; only fishermen in small boats casting their lines near the shore.

Brian and I drove the pontoon to the center and Blue Sky waved enthusiastically. As we pulled up, I could see Blue Sky's expensive camera resting in his lap.

"I took pictures of the sunrise," he explained as the boat pulled up next to his kayak.

It was impossible to be angry at Blue Sky. Even Brian was laughing at the situation as he leaned over the rail to hand him a life jacket.

"Blue Sky, you have to have a life jacket when you're in any boat," he said. Blue Sky willingly took it and promised Brian he'd wear one from then on.

The July Fourth weekend included a celebration of the independence of the United States. Fireworks were part of the evening, and Blue Sky set up his tripod to capture the show. He had taken pictures of everything: fish swimming under the pier, a large bird landing on the neighbor's bench, Murphy shaking water off after a swim, and the flames of the bonfire. His fascination with everything made me appreciate the place more.

As we dropped him off at the train on Sunday evening, he could not have been more appreciative to the entire family. He hugged Marlene and kissed Murphy's head before leaving. I felt a little guilty for taking it all for granted.

The next week, Blue Sky informed me he wanted to take his camera and capture the nighttime skyline of the city. On Saturday night, we headed to the lakefront. I was worried as we walked behind the Shedd Aquarium to a grassy area on the shore of Lake Michigan. I was sure we were trespassing.

"No one will care," he said as he looked around. "If they come, we will just pretend we are tourists and say we are sorry."

I was learning to navigate the city by helping Blue Sky, who always went in the wrong direction. The freedom I had felt like when I was living with the guys under the bridge, only without the fear of constant hunger.

For the next few months, we spent all our time together. Of course, we were together at school, but we'd also hang out on weekends. Marlene was happy I had made a friend my age, someone with whom I could connect.

By fall, we were taking our next set of tests. This time, Blue Sky passed me by. He skipped into TOEFL test prep, but I had to take an additional writing course. That meant we would only see each other outside of classes.

"Maybe I can be on the beach in California before it snows," he said as he held up his practice test score.

The TOEFL prep course prepared us for the framework of how the test was administered and what to expect from the questions. In November, Blue Sky passed his test. And that meant he would leave for the West Coast. When he told me, I realized just how much I would miss him.

In her emails and conversations, it was clear how Eva missed NPH. Her cheerful outlook was changing. She said the classes were hard and the girls in the dorm were in different programs and had different interests. She felt alone. Her roommate was older and had friends of her own, and one of the girls from NPH had already quit. I wished I could see her but knew even if I were in El Salvador, with no way to travel, I would only be able to connect with her on Face-Time anyway.

Blue Sky and I went out to lunch on his final week when he asked, "So Sam, what is your dream? It's time for you to decide so when you pass the test you are ready."

I explained that I had spoken to Marlene about studying computers. I loved to help Brian with his phone and the computer at home. I also helped set up Matt's new school computer. I didn't know what else to tell him. "I guess, computers."

"Don't sound so excited," he laughed and slapped my shoulder. "You've got to embrace it. What's the worst thing that could happen?"

What's the worst thing that could happen? I thought about it for weeks and started to feel anxious. Fear climbed into my jaw. Perhaps the Byrnes would not want me anymore. I could fail and disappoint everyone, both here and in El Salvador. Maybe Eva would find someone new and wouldn't want me. What if I ended up back under the bridge? Worse yet, what if I ended up in jail? Would I ever be able to embrace what was next without being afraid?

The idea of dreaming seemed silly.

32

On to College
Sam

I FOUND MYSELF WRITING Eva more often after Blue Sky left for California. He promised to stay in touch and said he would visit, but I did not expect to ever see him again. I had seen Los Angeles in the movies. The weather was perfect and only rich, beautiful people lived there. Blue Sky would fit right in and never look back. Why would he come back to Chicago?

I was sitting in the lobby of the English Academy watching two new Chinese students take a tour. They looked nervous. Neither smiled. It made me realize how the eighteen months here had changed me.

Anders came bounding out of his office to deliver the news. I had passed the TOEFL test and could enroll at a university to begin studying for my degree. The plan was to finish English classes in December and begin studies at Northeastern Illinois University in January 2014.

The next week, Marlene and I took part in new student orientation and toured the NEIU campus. Nothing about the experience was as welcoming as the English Language Academy. The students were walking to their classes alone, the place was too big, and the foreign student office was in a basement in a building far from the center of campus. My counselor was a young man named Will who seemed disorganized and aloof. I was happy to have months before classes started.

In November, Father Ron visited Chicago and seemed excited to hear about my progress. He also brought news about Jose.

"Jose will be studying in the U.S. too," he announced. "Olegario was able to secure a scholarship for a special study abroad program at the University of Iowa. Jose will learn about agriculture."

Father Ron explained that Iowa was a long way from Chicago, but at a minimum, he wanted me to reach out and help him transition. Jose would arrive in late December and stay with a family during the 10-month exchange program.

After a simple "graduation" in the lobby of the English Language Academy, I spent my second Christmas with the Byrnes. I missed Eva but still loved everything about this holiday and its traditions: Christmas mass, decorating the tree, lighting the outside of the house, the big meals, and of course, opening gifts.

Matt and I carried bins of decorations down from the attic and began unwrapping the figurines and ornaments. The house slowly filled with nativity scenes, snowmen, and Santa statues. Murphy seemed excited and was sniffing everything. Holiday music filled the air. Marlene surprised me with a green stocking embroidered with "Samuel" on it to place with the other family stockings on the fireplace.

Staring at the stockings on the lighted fireplace, I realized just how much they all cared for me. I was feeling anxious about school and longing for home to be with Eva, but there was a place in my heart for them too.

On my first day of college, I felt prepared. It was cold at the bus stop, but I knew the route. The commute was shorter than the one to DePaul. I memorized the map and knew all the names of the buildings at NEIU by heart.

Even with all my preparation, I ended up walking around confused. I found my first classroom, took a seat in the back, and folded up the map. It was Sociology 101, whatever that meant. A week ago, we bought my books so I could start reading ahead. I was convinced everyone would be smarter than me and thought being prepared would help me keep up with the other students.

After class, I went for my first adviser appointment. The woman at the front desk pointed to a tiny office and told me to go in and wait. I sat down in the chair next to the door and put my backpack under my seat so it wouldn't get in the way and trip the counselor. The office was small but had photos and art lined up on the desk and a ledge along the window. I noticed a beautiful piece of pottery, full of colors, which reminded me of home.

A man burst into the room, startling me. "I am Luis Ortiz." His energy reminded me of Doctor Patel.

"Samuel Antonio Jimenez Coreas," he read aloud as he opened a file folder and sat down. "This transcript says you are from El Salvador and went to DePaul English Language Academy. Tell me about yourself."

"Yes. That is me. I am here to study computers," I replied.

"I see that. But tell me about *you*," he said again.

I didn't understand. He sat back and waited, looking straight at me with a big smile. I felt compelled to talk.

"I came from NPH—Nuestros Pequeños Hermanos—and went to high school in El Salvador," I said.

"What is NPH?" he asked. I could tell he was honestly interested.

I told him my whole story, from the beginning. How I was found by Jorge and lived with his family. How I went to the first orphanage and ran away, living on the streets. How I arrived at NPH and it soon felt like home. How I had come to the United States with Juan. I even told him about Blue Sky.

It all just flowed out of me to this man, a stranger, who nodded and looked squarely into my eyes. I wasn't sure why, but he seemed familiar, and it felt good to get it all out.

"That's quite a story, and you have accomplished much," he said. "I think you will do just fine here, and I will be right by your side along the way to make sure you have success."

He told me about himself. He was Mexican and had come from immigrant parents. Their dream was for him to study and get his degree in the US, just like me. He spent time going over my schedule, making sure I knew how to get to my classes. He explained what a syllabus was and how hard I would need to study.

"Sam, I want you to do something for me," he said. "My Latino students have a habit of being too quiet in class. They don't raise their hands or press the teachers if they don't understand. They don't always ask for what they need. I worry that you may fall into that category as well."

I nodded, and he continued. "I want you to take part in the lectures. Promise me you will sit in the first two rows of each classroom. Ask questions. Be confident. Let the teachers know who you are. It will help later when you have questions or problems. And sometimes, that level of participation can even mean a better grade for you."

I left the campus feeling empowered. I wished Blue Sky were with me so I could tell him about it.

33

School

Sam

MY FIRST MONTH AT NEIU was quite different from my time at DePaul. The campus was big and I kept getting lost. I had the map open all the time to navigate to my classrooms. I had been late to many classes and had bought the wrong book for one class. I struggled to understand everything the teachers said in those first few days. They talked so fast I couldn't write quickly enough to capture it in my notes.

The students at NEIU kept to themselves. One teacher announced she would not assign group projects, explaining she understood it was a "commuter school" and hard for students to meet. So, our interactions were short—we would talk before class about the assignments and deadlines, listen to the lecture, and then leave campus.

I missed Anders. I missed Blue Sky. I even missed the new foreign students awkwardly starting their first few days at the Academy. Here, I seemed to be the awkward one.

The students were constantly on their phones, having conversations, and laughing. They were always in a hurry, getting their work done on campus and leaving. Most of the time, I was too afraid to engage for fear I'd be wrong with my answers.

Eva's communication became less frequent. She was always busy or just didn't want to talk. I was worried she was unhappy, yet there was consolation in knowing studying in El Salvador was not easy either.

By the end of February, I was exhausted. I'd sit on the bus to and from school, leaning my forehead on the cool glass of the window. On my first day, I noticed a man on the street, and I looked for him every day. I chose my seat on the south side so I could get a good look at him as we passed. He was obviously homeless, living under a bridge. Dirty and thin but not old. He had a backpack full of stuff and a blanket folded and tucked away in the concrete cubby space he appeared to have secured as his own.

On the first day, I barely caught a glimpse of him, but each day after, I noticed something new about him. He had a cover to protect his things on rainy days. He kept his water bottle in the same place on the cement ledge. There was a book next to it. He reminded me of the days I had lived under the bridge. I wondered where those guys were now. Could they still be living on the streets? Was someone new occupying my spot under our bridge? What had happened to the few items I had left behind?

At times, I belonged in that world more than this one. It seemed like a long time ago and yet familiar, like yesterday.

Jose was the one bright spot. He arrived in Iowa and received a new cell phone. We started to talk and text, working on a plan to see each other.

"I have something to talk to you about," I said to Brian and Marlene one evening. I explained how Jose was studying in Iowa and asked if he could visit.

A few nights later, I sat listening to Marlene talk with Jose's host mother. She answered question after question about where Jose would be staying, who would chaperone his activities, and how he would travel to and from Iowa. Visiting people was highly unusual for students in his exchange program.

In the end, Marlene convinced her that Jose would be safe, and the woman agreed to the visit. I was thrilled. I couldn't wait to see him and show him around Chicago.

34

Guys' Day Out
Sam

JOSE ARRIVED AT THE bus depot with one small backpack. Waving my arms, I yelled his name so loud that a baby in a stroller next to me started to cry.

Brian drove us home silently as we caught up in Spanish.

"How is your school?" I asked.

"It's good. We are from all different countries—Guatemala, Honduras, Mexico, and even Brazil—and coming together to study agriculture," he explained. "Olegario entered NPH into the program and offered the spot to me."

"I didn't know you wanted to be a farmer," I said.

"I don't," he explained timidly. "But I was working on the farm at NPH when the grant approval came in and wanted the chance to study here."

I thought about how difficult it was for any of us to answer the question, "What do you want to do?" We just wanted to live, to eat, to survive. We didn't think about lifelong aspirations like other people.

"Do you like computers?" he asked.

"Yes, of course. But I don't know if I will like studying computers in class," I said, glad Brian couldn't understand Spanish. Up to that point, I hadn't told him or Marlene about my doubts.

"What is happening at NPH?" I was desperate to know everything.

Eva and I were talking with still less frequency. She said it was because of school. She told me her grades were fine, but I could sense her interest in and dedication to school declining.

"Let's see. Olegario is the same," he said. "Luis had an accident with the car. Someone hit him and the car needed repairing. You can't even ask him about it, he is so angry. We repainted the school."

I hung on every word. I could picture it as if I were there. The older kids with paint brushes and buckets. They were laughing as they moved across the walls making the school rooms bright and clean with a new coat of paint. They would have Luis yelling about spilled paint and demanding they clean up the mess. I could imagine his anger at wrecking his beloved car. He never liked it when I drove because he was always afraid something bad would happen.

"Don't you want to know about Eva?" he asked as he poked an elbow into my side.

"Yes, but we talk and write often," I said casually, not letting on that we weren't really communicating as much anymore.

"I was talking to someone at the college house about two weeks ago," he said. "Two of the girls have already quit school. They left soon after the first exam. One left for a boyfriend and no one knows why or where the other one went."

I was surprised. I hadn't imagined any of the kids quitting. For so much of our lives, we did whatever we were told. In college, students needed to keep their grades up or they were out. If they didn't want to stay, they could go. But they wouldn't just leave school; they'd be out of NPH as well. They were too old to return to the orphanage. It meant they'd be on their own.

It made me sad to think of any of us moving on—leaving NPH and going out into the world to fend for ourselves. How would those girls survive? Where would they live? How would they get money?

"How is Iowa?" I asked.

"My program focuses on agricultural practices that we can use back home. We study ways to grow more and better crops. What to do when the weather becomes an issue. Rain. Drought. That kind of stuff," he said.

"Do you like the other students?"

He thought for a second, "It's interesting. At home, we might have issues between our countries, but at school, we all get along. The countries don't seem to matter."

"I felt that way at DePaul," I said. "A friend of mine, Blue Sky—yes, that was what we called him—was from China. I could never imagine being a friend to someone like him before I got here, yet we had so much in common."

"Father Ron told me I had to be open to my classmates," Jose said.

"I got that same speech," I said and we both laughed.

"I live with a family and one other student," Jose continued. "He is from Chile, and his family owns a big farm there. He is more into school than I am."

We spent the evening catching up and made plans to explore the city. I was excited to show him my skills at navigating from the bus to the train and then to the city and out of Union Station.

Jose was amazed by Chicago. He loved everything: the buildings, the riverwalk, the lakeshore. We must have walked twenty miles in one day.

Dunkin Donuts became his favorite place. We stopped at the first one right off the train and then as we walked around, he noticed them everywhere. I never realized there were so many in downtown Chicago. Jose had eaten six donuts by noon.

The weekend went too fast, and Sunday night, we were back at the bus station dropping Jose off at the terminal.

"Jose, I want you to go straight into the bus terminal, through the ticket counter, and right to your gate," Brian warned as we drove into the city. "Sometimes, bad guys hang around outside."

We pulled up in front of Union Station and said our goodbyes. Jose crossed the street and as he was entering the building, a strange man went up to him and started talking. Before I knew what was happening, Brian was making a U-turn and pulling the car over to the curb.

"Stay in the car and move it if anyone comes," he said. "Keep your phone on." He hopped out of the car and jogged up to where Jose and the man were talking.

Brian simply grabbed Jose by the elbow and moved him into the building. They disappeared as the man yelled something at their backs. I locked the doors and waited, looking behind me for the police or someone to tell me to move the car.

Brian returned. "Sam, talking to guys like that can get you robbed or worse. You should never engage."

I looked back as we drove off. The man was still standing outside the station. I wondered who his next victim would be.

35

Fall Back to School
Sam

THE FALL SEMESTER STARTED with a music class. It fulfilled an elective requirement, and Luis thought I needed something easier and less "academic" to reduce my stress level.

I walked into the classroom behind who I soon learned was the teacher. He looked like a student; young, with long hair and dressed in casual clothes with sandals.

"I'm Mr. Bruin," he explained. "I will be taking you through the introduction to music, including an understanding of notes and composition."

I sat down in the back of the room and started to settle in. Around me, the students had long, skinny white instruments sitting in front of them.

"We will play a simple instrument, called a recorder, to learn about notes and musical timing," he said. "If you haven't bought a recorder yet, please have one by the next class."

I sat through the whole class knowing there was no way I could play that instrument or understand one thing he was saying. In the first thirty minutes, I decided to drop the class. When he announced a bathroom break, I left and never returned.

The next day, I went to Luis' office to switch to another class. I wanted to have it settled before letting Marlene and Brian know.

Luis saw me coming. "Sammy, my man, how is your first week going?" he asked with his usual enthusiasm.

I explained my fear of the music class and told him I wanted to drop it. Without hesitation, he pulled out a large book listing all the classes for the semester. It was an easy change, and I chose "Introduction to Cinema" which fit my schedule perfectly. It also meant I would not have any classes on Friday.

After the appointment with Luis, I had two hours before my next class. I went to the cafeteria and sat at a long table near the door. Students were working together on projects, while others talked and laughed as they waited for their next class. I never talked to anyone.

Even in my classes, I sat quietly waiting for the teacher to begin the lecture. One day, a classmate asked me a question. I didn't understand and was afraid to ask him to repeat himself, so I just answered "no" and looked at my notebook. I made it clear to everyone that I wanted to be alone. And that is just what I was. Alone.

Last semester, I could have talked with Eva. She was fascinated by my classes and every aspect of the school, from the bus rides to the teachers. Lately, she had become distant. She was not explaining her days in detail. Instead, she was complaining about her grades, telling me she was lonely. Our calls became shorter and shorter.

I was consumed by confusion. Had I said something wrong? Was I asking too much of her?

Child Development was my favorite class. Growing up with 476 children made the material relevant. It was the only class where I sat toward the front, had opinions, and contributed to the discussion.

How could I have gotten a D on my first paper for this class? I sat looking at it while the teacher explained the significance of the work and what it meant to our final grade. My leg was bouncing up and down and the boy in front of me turned around with a scowl to let me know the movement was annoying him.

I could see the girl on the left ahead of me holding her paper with an A grade. She was smiling and looking at the few red corrections the teacher had made. My paper had notes in the margins, as well as corrections in the paragraphs. A girl behind me stared at her paper, covering the top with her hand. I assumed her grade was bad too.

After class, the teacher came over to the two of us. "If you want to discuss the edits on your paper, just come meet me during office hours," she said.

I nodded at her, jammed the paper into my backpack, and left.

That evening, I set the paper down on the kitchen snack bar while Marlene was cleaning up after dinner.

"I need to tell you bad news," I said.

Marlene walked over to look at the paper. Calmly, she paged through and read the red marks on each sheet.

"Sam, everyone gets a bad grade in college," she explained. "That is part of learning."

"I just don't understand what the professor wants me to say," I said.

"Why don't you ask her?"

I remembered Luis telling me to talk to the teachers. I never did. This time, I knew it was necessary to ask for help.

The next day, I poked my head into the classroom early, hoping she would be alone. She wasn't there. One lone girl, the one with the A grade who constantly asked questions, was reading at her desk. I sat in my usual seat and waited.

The room was half full by the time our teacher arrived. I would have to wait until after class to talk with her. It meant I would miss my bus.

I sat through the class, barely concentrating, too sad to really care about the paper or even my grade. Eva had not written or called in three weeks. I tried to FaceTime her day after day but there was never an answer. Even my emails sat quietly in a row on my phone. I checked them constantly.

On Sunday night, I talked with Jose. He seemed quiet too and started telling me how he was finishing his studies in September and would go back to El Salvador.

"Will you continue college when you get home?" I asked. I expected he'd live at the NPH college house. I wished I could go with him.

"No."

"But why? What will you do?" I asked.

"I am going to get a job and work," he replied.

"Where?"

"One of the guys has a job at a call center and is renting an apartment. I think I'm finished with school and studying," Jose said, and then whispered. "One thing I know for sure is that I am not going to be a farmer. I hate this program." He laughed and I could feel his relief, like a huge burden was lifting.

I, on the other hand, felt worse than ever. At NEIU—and with both Jose and Eva—it felt like I was being left behind.

I was in a fog the whole week. I felt so disconnected from my life. NPH seemed so far away. The kids, the family I had grown up with, were leaving and spreading out in the world.

I had not heard from Eva.

On Sunday night, I called Jose again in desperation. I told him about Eva's silence. He promised to try to find something out.

I lied to Brian and Marlene when they asked if I was okay. I stared straight ahead in my classes, not taking notes. I lied about having to study when Mel and Mary Jo invited me for dinner.

The girl with the bad paper in our Child Development class tried to talk with me. I knew she was looking to discuss what we might do about our grades.

"Did you see the professor about your paper?" she asked.

"No." I didn't want to talk about it. She never spoke to me again.

A week later, I was in my room, and my phone lit up with Face-Time. It was Eva!

"How are you?" I asked with a big smile. I was desperate to talk to her. I wanted to tell her about Jose. I wanted to make her laugh about the music class because she knew I could not play an instrument. I wanted her to tell me it would all be okay. I needed her encouragement.

"I have to tell you something," she said. I knew something was wrong.

"What?"

She took a deep breath and spoke slowly. "I have left school."

"Why? Has something happened?"

"No. I just don't want to be a nurse anymore."

I couldn't understand. It had been her dream. "But—"

"Sam, I am seeing someone else."

There it was. The end.

"Who? Why?" I was so devastated that I couldn't form a sentence.

"Sam, you have a whole new life. I am here and lonely. I met someone and we are together. I have to be with him."

"But what about our plans? Our future?"

"They were just the plans of two young kids who knew nothing about life. Sam, you are a good man, and I will always . . ." She started crying, *sobbing* in fact, and couldn't finish her sentence.

"I don't understand. Something doesn't feel right. How could this happen?" I realized how fast I was talking, the questions racing out of my mouth.

"It just did. There is nothing to be done."

"Tell me why?" I begged.

"I can't," she replied through her tears. "I need to go. Take care of yourself, Sammy."

"Wait—"

But she was gone. I was paralyzed. My arms tingled. It was shock. It was as if my heart broke in two. All of this had been for us, for our future. And it was all gone in a matter of minutes. Nothing made sense.

For weeks, I walked around in a daze. At home, I told Marlene and Brian that I had lots of homework to give me an excuse to stay in my room. I was just staring at the pages of an open textbook.

I reached out to Jose, who was back in El Salvador, and told him about Eva. He was the only one who could offer any advice and help me find out what was going on. He knew the girls in the NPH school program and said he would talk with them to get more information.

Two weeks later, Jose called on FaceTime.

"I don't have much to tell you," he said. "No one knows why she left school, but they did say she was seeing a guy from the town. He is not from NPH or school. No one seems to know much about him. Even the girls were surprised when they found out."

I asked myself over and over, *Why would she choose to date a random guy and risk our future?*

I tried to FaceTime her three times, but she never answered. She ignored my messages as well. Was it really over? I couldn't imagine a future without her in it.

The next set of grades proved I was not going to be successful at school. I had to go back to El Salvador, and I needed to find the right time to let everyone know.

At night, I dreamed of going home and finding Eva. I would walk up to her at NPH just like I had that first day. She would be so happy, throw her arms around my neck, and we would confess how hard it was in college. We would decide it was okay, that we didn't need big jobs or money if we had each other. Just like Jorge and Rosa, we would build a life and family together. Simple but happy is how I envisioned our future . . . our life.

I called Jose to let him know I had decided to come home. We started making plans. He was excited to have a friend to live with and was sure he could get me a job interview at the call center. I felt like things were falling into place. I was one step closer to my life with Eva.

Sundays at the Byrnes were spent together. As a family, we went to Mass in the morning. Sometimes there were baseball games or other afternoon activities, and then dinner. Today, it was bowling.

Maggie would heave the ball from between her legs and it would roll slowly down the lane. Most times, it would lean to the left or the right and end up in the gutter.

"Let me show you how," Matt said as he tossed the ball down the lane as hard as he could with the same result.

"Ha, you got a gutter ball too," Maggie laughed.

I liked these times. It had felt so comfortable, like I was meant to be there, but today, it just felt sad.

I had a terrible stomachache knowing what I was about to do to them. It was time to drop the bomb and tell them I wanted to go home to El Salvador.

36

Return to El Salvador
Jorge

BACK IN THE AIRPORT, it was as if no time had passed since I last stood here watching Sam leave for the US. I was in the exact same place, looking at gate 27 and the board that listed a TACA flight arriving from Chicago.

The airport was busy but it didn't take long to find him. There he was, coming off the jetway. Sam looked different. Older. Intense. And I also saw a sense of relief on his face. What had happened to him? Why was he back?

The airport was familiar to both of us. All the faces and people. There was a family pushing piles of luggage away from baggage claim. A little boy was draped over a big suitcase, riding it like it was a horse. He looked tired from a long trip. His mother carried a baby in her arms while she dragged him along. At baggage claim, an old man struggled to get his bag off the moving belt, and Sam stepped up to help him.

Then, as he waited for his bags, he looked around. Was he searching for a friendly face? As always, I wished he could see me.

But there was no one there. Not even an NPH driver. He was alone, quitting school, and too old to return to the orphanage.

However, Sam had a sense of confidence I hadn't seen before. He seemed calm and focused. After he grabbed two suitcases, he headed to the cab line. On a sheet of paper, he read off the name and address of a small motel. He had a reservation for two nights.

At the little motel, Sam registered with an old man who sat behind a thick plexiglass window. Sam got his key, rolled his suitcases down the walkway to room 12, and carefully locked the door behind him. The motel room was small and simple: a double bed with an old green bedspread, a nightstand, and a lamp with a hole in the shade from being knocked over. The bathroom, with a ripped shower curtain, was small as well. But none of that seemed to matter to Sam. He was on his own, charting his next course, and that's what mattered. Besides, he'd lived in much worse conditions.

He lifted his suitcase onto the bed, pulled out his iPad, and connected to Wi-Fi. Sam was relieved when Jose answered his FaceTime call. They planned to meet in the morning; Jose already had rentals for them to tour and was sure they would find an apartment quickly. Jose also told him about the job interview at the call center and said he would get it scheduled.

"Christian wants to live with us too," he said.

Christian, another *pequeño* from NPH, had aged out and was working at a tire factory. He was sleeping on the floor at a friend's house and needed a permanent place to live.

"That's fantastic," Sam replied. He loved the idea of having roommates. "Will he come with us tomorrow?"

"No. He doesn't get any time off work."

Sam hung up the phone and smiled at the idea of the three of them having a place together.

Feeling free, Sam took a long shower and pulled out the granola bars Marlene had packed in his bag. He found a note wrapped around one of the bars and opened it. His smile told me it was Marlene reminding him that he was not alone. He carefully folded the paper and tucked it under the clothes in his bag.

The next morning, Sam stood looking up and down the long marble corridor of a local shopping mall. When he and Jose saw each other, they embraced like old friends, together again. Their excitement and connection made me happy. *This will be Sam's next family*, I thought.

Over coffee, they talked about their plans. To save money, they would shop at the food market rather than buy anything from the mall restaurants. Jose had information about two rentals near the call center. They could take the bus to work. He also had an appointment for Sam to meet with his boss later in the week.

The boys discussed living costs but had no idea how to budget. They would have to pay for electricity. "What do you think that costs?" Jose asked.

Sam shrugged.

Bus fare was also a concern. They would need to save enough money to get to work and back. It was all a bit scary, but I could tell it felt liberating for them to be in control of their own lives.

Sam let Jose know that he had a stash of money Brian had given him before he left. "We can get started with that," he said.

"How did they take it when you told them you were leaving?" Jose asked.

"It was hard," Sam said. "I had to say goodbye to Murphy. Marlene took me to the airport. She was standing alone, crying, as I went through security." He remembered taking a last look back at her while waiting in line.

"They are nice people," Jose replied.

"Yes. It was hard to leave them. I hugged Murphy tighter and longer than the family," he said. "I even asked Marlene to promise Murphy would be alive at my next visit."

"You will see them again," Jose said.

Sam just looked at him as they packed up and left the mall. He wasn't so sure.

The first apartment tour was terrible. The house was dirty. The sink was hanging halfway off the wall in the kitchen. The windows had bars on them, and the neighborhood seemed dangerous.

As they approached the second house, a woman was waiting for them outside. She was young and looked as if they were late. When they got closer, she met them with a smile and quickly walked them into the house. The door was wide open.

This house had a big kitchen and a small table with two chairs sitting in the corner. She explained the people who had moved out left things behind that they could keep. Jose and Sam smiled at each other. It was their first furniture, and it was free. The house was simple but perfect, with one bathroom, a kitchen, a small sitting area and two bedrooms.

At the end of the tour, the boys stood in the main room with the woman who explained they would need to leave a cash deposit of $400 to hold the house. They could move in the next day. When Jose asked about the lease, she explained that she would bring it with the keys the next morning.

Sam looked at Jose and shrugged, "I only brought $250."

Jose had nothing.

The woman stared at them for a moment and then said, "I guess I'll take it."

She was not happy, but when she accepted, Jose and Sam looked at each other and smiled. They made plans for Sam to meet her at the house the next morning to get the keys. The boys stood outside on the street after the woman left.

"What do you think?" Sam asked.

"The perfect bachelor pad," Jose replied as they smiled and bumped fists.

They walked to the bus stop and discussed what items to buy when they had money. Their needs were simple: beds and maybe a few pieces of furniture.

Sam woke up the next morning and practically jumped out of bed. He had a little food left from the trip and decided to wait to share it with Jose at dinner. Dragging his suitcases, he checked out of the hotel and loaded his belongings onto the bus. He would meet the woman to get the keys, and Jose would come home after his shift. *Home.* It sounded good to Sam.

Sam arrived early and placed his things under a tree in the front yard while he waited. At about noon, he started checking his watch. He walked around the house to check the doors. They were shut and locked. No one was around.

By three p.m., I had a terrible feeling that Sam and Jose had been tricked. Sam was starting to recognize their mistake, and when Jose showed up just before five, he was in a panic.

"What are you doing?" Jose yelled from down the street.

"She never showed up."

"What do you mean 'she never showed up'?" He looked up and down the street just as Sam had a thousand times.

"She never showed up," he repeated.

Jose walked around the house then went to the house next door and knocked.

"Hello," he said. The man cracked the door open an inch and peeked out. "Do you know the woman who rents out this house?" he asked, pointing.

"There is no woman," the man answered. "The old man died."

"Old man? But a woman showed it to us yesterday. She told us we could rent it," Jose insisted.

"No. It has been vacant for months. I don't know anything more." Then he slammed the door in Jose's face.

They were realizing that they had been swindled. In desperation, they stood on the front lawn checking the street again. Finally, reality set in.

"What do we do now? I checked out of the motel," Sam said, looking at the pile under the tree.

"I gave my room at the apartment to someone else. They're just holding my stuff until I go and get it," Jose said.

"And the money's gone."

They were homeless.

"Now what?" Jose asked.

Sam had no idea. There was no one to help them. No family. No Jorge. No more NPH.

"The motel," was all Sam said as he started gathering his stuff.

Jose helped Sam with his things, and they trudged back down the street.

Sam checked back in and shut the door to room twelve. He remembered the food he had and dug in his bag, handing a granola bar to Jose as he sat down next to him on the bed. Thank goodness Marlene had insisted on sending food along with him.

They were deflated and scared. How could they have been so stupid?

As they replayed the house tour with the woman, they started to see the clues.

"Why didn't we notice the door was wide open?" Jose asked, under his breath. "She never used a key to get in."

"She must have broken in before we arrived," Sam said. "Why didn't we get her name and ask for identification?"

"Do you think she was working with someone?"

Sam looked down at his granola bar and said, "I'll call Marlene and Brian." It was the only thing he could think to help.

Sam FaceTimed Brian and explained what happened. Sam knew he was angry, not at them—at the thief. Marlene was behind him, looking worried and trying to reassure him that things could be worse. "At least you only gave her $250," she said. "And you weren't hurt."

Brian told Sam he would send him some more money to start over. He also told him to go to the police and report the incident.

The next morning at the police station, an officer listened to Sam's story. He told Sam the woman was most likely long gone, and even if they did find her, she probably would not have their money. The whole thing felt like a waste of time.

Jose was making better progress. He found another apartment, and this time, the boys were careful to get a lease, take the man's name, and agreed to pay him only when they got the keys.

The place was simple. Two bedrooms, a bathroom with a sink, toilet, and shower stall, and a large room with a sink under the window. Otherwise, it was bare. No furniture. No refrigerator. No stove. Nothing.

But none of it mattered because it was a fresh start.

The next morning, they moved in, trudging their life's belongings off the bus to the house. Sam placed his clothes in neat, folded stacks on top of the big suitcase, using it like a table. He reached into the other bag and pulled out two blankets, two towels, and a small pillow.

Jose came into the room, holding up a roll of toilet paper. "I brought this from the hotel," he said.

"Marlene packed blankets and towels for us," Sam said. He handed one of each to Jose. They would serve as beds until something else could be found.

Sam laid the blanket down and was staring up at the cracked ceiling, thinking about the places his life had taken him. As he lay there, I started to think about his little blanket in Diego's closet all those years ago. Then, I thought how different this place was from the Byrnes' house and the big bed he had in Chicago.

On the third night, Christian arrived. He had a simple duffel bag with clothes. Together, the boys start scavenging the streets for discarded items they could use at the house. They found a broken kitchen table (which they were able to repair) and a lamp. It had no lampshade, but they couldn't afford to be fussy. Their collection of kitchen chairs came one by one in different shapes and sizes. They bought a simple shower curtain and were saving to get beds. For the kitchen, they used plastic forks, knives, and cups from restaurants; their dishes were leftover plastic containers.

Within weeks, Sam confessed his plans to find out about Eva.

"I need to know what happened and where she is," he said.

Jose and Christian understood. He asked them to reach out to anyone for information. Both agreed. Perhaps the older NPH *pequeños,* working in Santa Ana, knew something.

Sam interviewed well and secured a job at the call center, just as Jose had predicted. His client was Hotels.com, and for the first month, he was in training to learn how to help customers calling with reservation issues. The call center office was a warehouse with tables and computers arranged in long rows. Sam had an old chair that tilted to one side and creaked when he tapped his foot.

His first call was from a family in Manchester, New Hampshire. The man explained that they'd just arrived to check into their room but the attendant at the hotel front desk told them it was full. Sam did exactly as he was trained: apologize, rebook them, and send them to another nearby hotel.

Most callers were irritated and it didn't take long to realize the call center was designed to find customers other hotels or rebook them; refunds were not part of the deal. Learning to manage the issues—and not escalating the call to a supervisor—was the goal.

Job performance was checked and rated based on how well they managed each situation. Sam's English skills were well above most of the staff and the manager took to him at once.

It wasn't a great job, but Sam was happy. After two weeks, he received his paycheck and was in control for the first time in his life. Jose and Sam spent time figuring out a budget: rent, food, and even an allowance to get a six-pack of beer.

If Sam and Jose were poor, Christian had nothing. Because he was not bilingual, his job options were bleak. He found work in a tire factory and spent his days moving tires with his bare hands. He was paid little and only worked as they needed him, always scraping for more hours.

He shared a room with Jose, and they let him pay what he could afford for rent.

Christian's on-again, off-again work schedule came in handy when the small refrigerator was delivered. Brian and Marlene had insisted on buying it as a "housewarming" gift, whatever that meant. I'd never heard of such a thing but knew it would make a dramatic difference for the boys. They shared everything, and being able to keep food cold would help tremendously.

Christian was always the last one home, working long hours at the tire factory. One Friday evening, they were waiting for him, anxious to see him.

Exhausted and dirty, Christian went into the bathroom to wash up. When he came out, the boys were waiting for him in the kitchen.

"We have something for you," Jose said.

"We went in on it together," Sam added.

Christian looked down and saw a paper bag sitting on his chair. He walked over, looked at them suspiciously, and dug inside. He pulled out a pair of canvas gloves.

"For me?"

"Yes," Jose replied.

"We thought you might like them for work," Sam said.

The skin on Christian's hands was cracked and often bled from cuts and scrapes he got while moving the tires around in the factory.

He stared at the gloves with gratitude on his face. The boys knew no one ever looked after Christian, not even as a child. He rarely spoke of his family story. Even at NPH, Christian had been the quiet kid who never demanded anything of anyone. He never expected anything, either.

"Thank you so much," Christian said.

Before it got too emotional, Jose said, "Look in the bag again."

Christian pulled out a six-pack of beer and smiled. They laughed as he handed each a bottle.

37

Finding Eva
Sam

I DIDN'T TELL JOSE or Christian about my plan. One of the girls living at the NPH house had messaged me on Facebook with information about Eva. I read it over and over, yet I still couldn't believe it.

Eva had met him at the college. He worked in one of the cafeterias and she would see him every day. They only talked at first, but then started to eat together, and soon he was taking her out in the evenings. The rumor was they were living in a small town called Chalchuapa.

I researched the weekend schedule and took the bus to what I assumed was the center of town. I walked around the city, concentrating on people's faces, desperate to find Eva. I came upon a white church with a beautiful wooden entry and walked up to read the sign. It was a Catholic Church consecrated to the patron of the city of Santiago Apostol; a statue of a man on horseback was on the dome. I looked up to ask for help in my search.

I found a small restaurant on the main street. I ordered coffee and watched people go in and out of the market. I spent two hours before deciding to walk the streets again.

Once, I thought I saw her. I practically jumped out of my skin, and ran down the street. The woman disappeared at the corner, and I thought I had lost her. I ran around the corner of a building and stopped in my tracks. She was five feet away, talking to an old woman in a doorway. I must have startled them because they both looked spooked. I froze. I realized it wasn't Eva, apologized, and hurried away. After a full day, I gave up.

Two weeks later, I returned. I walked up and down the streets, stopping at a café to eat lunch. I ordered a *pupusa* and water and sat for a long time. The server kept coming over to see if I wanted anything else, rolling her eyes each time I politely said no.

It was a busy day at the market. Families coming and going. An old lady pulled a wagon with her grocery bags. It looked heavy and it made me want to help.

As I paid the cashier, I felt a strange sensation. Instinctively, I looked up.

There she was. Eva.

She was walking toward me with two bags of groceries clutched to her chest. She looked the same—beautiful brown eyes on a quiet, friendly face. She smiled at an old woman. I finished paying and hid behind a group of people waiting to be seated until she passed. She never saw me.

I followed her up the street. She ambled past a car shop and up a hill toward the bus stop. I walked quickly, not wanting the bus to come before I could reach her.

When she arrived at the bus stop, she put the bags on the bench, turned to the side and placed both hands on her lower back.

She was pregnant.

How could that be? We had talked so many times about waiting to have sex until we were married. Being careful. Knowing we were not ready to start a family. How could she have done this?

Frozen in my thoughts, I watched the bus pull up and Eva grab her bags. It was as if everything was in slow motion. She got on the bus, paid her fare, and vanished down the aisle. She had no idea I was there. She never looked back.

I turned and slowly walked away.

38

Life
Jorge

AFTER FINDING EVA, SAM'S demeanor changed. I had never seen him so dejected and heavy-hearted.

It took him two weeks to tell Jose and Christian about it. The boys were enjoying Saturday night beers in the backyard after finding two old plastic chairs in the trash and dragging them to the house. Sam went outside, sat on the grass, and told them the whole story.

"So, you never talked to her?" Jose asked, shaking his head.

"Who needs a girl like that?" Christian blurted out.

Both had suspected Eva might be pregnant but neither dared to bring it up. They knew Sam would be crushed, and they were worried about him.

"No, she never saw me," Sam said. "I wanted to run up and talk to her, but my body froze. I have thought about going back to that street every day since."

"I don't think anything good will come of that," Jose said, looking to Christian for support.

"What would you do if you did see her? What if she wanted to get back with you now?" Christian asked.

Sam stared into space. "I don't know," he replied, almost talking to himself. "I can't help her now. I think I should leave her alone . . . with him."

"I think it's best," Jose agreed.

The realization that the life he dreamed about with Eva was gone left an empty place in his soul. His conversations with Blue Sky about dreams haunted him. His dreams had always revolved around her, and now there was nothing. More than sad, he felt dead inside.

At work, Sam became driven. It was all he had. His boss noticed his performance and complimented him on his abilities. He even used Sam as an example as two recruits toured the office for orientation.

"I'm going to try to become a manager," Sam told Jose one evening.

"That's ambitious," Jose replied, "but if anyone can do it, it's you."

Sam scheduled a meeting with his boss to discuss the options.

"Sam, our managers all have college degrees," he said as he looked over Sam's employment folder. "I see you *were* in college. Do you have plans to finish your studies?"

Sam shook his head.

That night, Sam began searching the internet for a new job. He knew he could not listen to people complain on the phone for the rest of his life.

The boys' lives became routine: work, home, eat, sleep, work . . . On weekends, Christian put in long hours and arrived home late. Jose and Sam didn't have anyone to visit, so they ventured out to the mall or the market on Saturday afternoons. Otherwise, they were at home.

One Friday, Jose announced he was seeing a girl.

"Who is she? How did you meet?" Sam asked.

Jose said she worked in his department and her name was Sofia.

"I am taking her out tomorrow night," he said, smiling and holding a shirt. "I am going to wash this and wear it for my date."

On Saturday, Sam found himself alone and wandering around the house. Christian was working. Jose was with Sophia. Sam decided to clean the kitchen and bathroom. He refolded his clothes and cleaned the refrigerator. Afterward, he surfed the internet for jobs. He looked at stories on Facebook. Everyone was having fun with friends and family except him.

Over the next few weeks, Jose and Sofia spent more time together. Sam was alone, missing his friend and missing Eva.

Brian and Marlene called at least every other Sunday. They asked about Sam's job, the house, and the other boys. Sometimes, Jose would get on to talk with them. On the calls, Sam was always upbeat, making his life sound great. He didn't want Marlene and Brian to worry, so he did his best to hide how he really felt.

He confessed to Jose that he was having trouble sleeping because he was still thinking about Eva. Sometimes, he said, when he could sleep, he dreamed about her; happy dreams where they'd get married and start a family together. But then he'd wake up . . . alone.

After a long pause, Sam asked, "Do you think Eva would have gotten pregnant if I had stayed in El Salvador? Is this because of me?"

Jose simply shrugged. "Maybe it's time you chase another dream."

Sam knew he was right. It was time to move on.

39

Dead Bodies

Sam

EIGHT MONTHS. THAT'S HOW long it had been since I returned to El Salvador. I continued to do well at my job. I received a raise for my excellent work and was reassigned to the Travelocity account. As one of the few people who had personal experience traveling through airports and staying in hotels, I jumped ahead of my peers.

My new assignment meant handling more complicated calls, although most were still from customers having issues with reservations while on a trip. From finding no reservation upon arrival at their hotel to being charged the wrong amount at checkout, callers were always angry. I was the second representative a caller would talk to, and my job was to resolve the issue without escalating or issuing a refund. We could offer options as a last resort but were trained to solve the problem in a way that would not cost the company any money.

I was able to talk to guests with little difficulty. My English was better than most, even Jose's. I was also a good problem-solver and remained polite while managing complaints. My boss liked my work. I hated it. With each passing day, the job weighed heavier on my shoulders.

One morning, a family called with an issue at a hotel in Orlando. It reminded me of a trip I took to Florida with the Byrnes. We rented a house, and "Nana" came along. She sat by the pool watching me, Matt, and Maggie swim. Brian played with us, cannonballing into the water, splashing us all, even Nana. The warmth and sunshine were a wonderful reprieve from the cold Chicago winter.

During our trip, we visited Disney World. The park was nothing like the little waterpark in El Salvador. The castle, the rides, and all the different villages were amazing. I still had the map we used to find our way around the park. It was folded up and tucked in the pocket of my suitcase.

I held onto a few treasures from my time in the US. Things like the stir stick from a drink at the Drake with Blue Sky and my tickets to a Cubs game. There were also three photos of the family, including one in the gardens outside the park entrance at Disney.

The most fun for me was the speedway. Brian, Matt, and I raced our cars and kept passing Marlene and Maggie.

I imagined my caller's family trip ruined by a mistake in the hotel reservation. It made me sad for them.

The only good part of the call center job was getting my paycheck every two weeks. It meant I had my own money that I could spend to live *my* life. Even though we were barely scraping by, we had our freedom, and it was a wonderful part of living on our own.

One Friday night, Sofia was busy and the three of us were having beers and talking.

"Do you have a dream?" I asked the guys.

"Do you mean, do I dream?" Jose asked. "Like when I sleep?"

"No," I said. "Do you have a dream? Something you want to accomplish in life, a goal for the future?"

He thought for a second, "No, not really. I guess this is my dream." He raised his beer.

Blue Sky was right. Dreams were not for everyone.

I felt like I should have one. Blue Sky had been clear about how important it was to dream. With this empty space in my life (and in my heart), the idea of having a dream seemed more pressing. I needed to replace Eva with something new, I just didn't know what.

Thoughts of my time with Blue Sky at DePaul, with Mel and Mary Jo at dinner, and with Maggie watching funny videos started to fill my head. On the bus ride to and from work, I would daydream about my time in Chicago, and with my U.S. "family," and it made me happy, even happier than when I was there. The memories seemed better somehow.

One afternoon on the bus ride home from work, I stared out the window and thought about the first time I went sledding. I remembered the frigid air and seeing my own breath. The wet snow. My cold, achy toes after hours outside. The feeling of acceleration as I flew down the hill on the sled. Cuddling up with Murphy to get warm after we got home.

I jerked back to reality as the bus came to a screeching halt. Before the driver could say anything, two men pushed open the door and rushed up the steps. They had guns, one to the driver's head and the other pointed at us passengers.

There had been rumors that gangs were robbing buses and killing bus drivers in retaliation for the government arresting gang members in a country-wide crackdown on crime. One of the thieves started down the aisle holding out a small sack and shaking down each passenger for money. Everyone was scrambling to get cash out of their pockets and purses.

The thief had a red handkerchief around his face, but tattoos down his neck were visible. The numerals XIII on his knuckles confirmed he was part of MS13. Everyone lived in fear of the group. They had a vicious reputation. For years, the police and government officials ignored their crimes and left them alone so their own families wouldn't be threatened. But the new leadership was cracking down and the gangs were retaliating with a vengeance.

I stayed quiet and still until he was at my seat and then dug everything out of my pocket to drop into the bag. I guess because I was young, he never questioned how little I contributed. I could feel my toes curl around the money hidden in my shoe, and I thought of Jorge and the green pouch. Was it worth trying to hide the cash? Would this thief know my trick?

Back up the aisle he went. Then, the two men forced the bus driver out of the bus. Everyone was afraid of what might happen next. The driver was on his knees in the dirt, terrified they would kill him. Instead, they beat him, leaving him bloody and face down on the side of the road before hopping back in their car and speeding off.

Once it was safe, a man ran to help the driver and I jumped from my seat. We turned him over and heard him wince in pain. I assumed his ribs were broken and knew by tomorrow he would have terrible black and blue bruises covering his face.

Lifting him gently, we sat him in the first row of the bus. An old woman walked up to offer him water and her handkerchief.

"What do we do now?" I asked the man.

"Can you drive?" he asked.

I shook my head. I didn't know how to drive a bus and was also afraid of being the next victim.

I wished Brian were there like at the train station in Chicago. He would know what to do.

Without hesitation, the man sat down, closed the door, and dropped the bus into gear. I sat in the front seat to navigate as he did his best to drive the massive beast. The old woman sat with the driver, trying to comfort him, but he was a mess both physically and emotionally.

Slowly, we got the bus back to the station and the man ran in to get help. I looked back at the driver, realizing he would never be safe going to work again. I decided to leave before the police arrived. I didn't want to get tangled up in reporting the criminals.

After catching another bus, I stepped off at my stop just like normal, only nothing about this felt normal. My knees were weak, yet I ran into the house. I just wanted to lock the door and feel safe again.

Jose was in the kitchen and noticed the blood on my shirt.

"What happened?"

I told him the whole story. He could hardly believe it. Until today, we thought these types of stories were rumors.

"I wonder what time Christian will get home?" he finally asked.

Our country had changed. We realized this violence was now our reality.

For the next few weeks, you could see and feel the fear on daily commutes. Women held their purses tighter. Men constantly looked around. Everywhere—on the bus, in the mall, and even at work—people were talking about the violence. We were all scared.

I remembered my bus rides in Chicago. The homeless man who no one seemed to bother. The people on the streets at night, laughing. Blue Sky and I on an evening adventure taking photos of the skyline. I could never do that here.

It was important for the government to stop the gangs, but retribution and violence were invading the entire community.

40

No Bus
Jorge

IT HAD BEEN MORE than six months since Sam laid eyes on Eva. I don't know what made him go back. It was a Saturday afternoon when he saw her. She was carrying a baby in her arms. She looked different. Messy. Her hair was in a tangled braid. Her clothes were different. She was distracted.

Trying to shop with a new baby looked difficult. She seemed agitated at the people around her, even the children. This was something Sam had never seen with the children at NPH; she had always been smiling and kind.

It was like he was seeing her life play out before his eyes, yet he was not part of it. At one point, it looked like he was going to move in to help her but stopped himself.

Following her through the market, he was careful not to be noticed. I knew he wouldn't talk to her, but he needed to see her one more time, one *last* time.

Sam was closing chapters in his life, and this was the most important one to finish. All the dreams they'd discussed had evaporated. They would never marry. There would be no family. They would not build a life together.

Did Eva regret giving up on her education or her dream to become a nurse? Did she love this guy more than Sam? She certainly didn't appear happier.

I wondered if she would be mad at Sam for giving up on his studies. Would she care about his dream now that she had given up on hers?

I caught a glimpse of the baby's face. I wasn't sure of its gender, but the child had Eva's beautiful eyes.

As Eva turned down the street, Sam stopped following her and watched her walk away. For a moment, he was sure she would turn around and see him. Instead, she adjusted her bags and moved on. He turned, walked back to the bus, and left for home. It was over.

Work had become more difficult. Because of his English skills, Sam was promoted to take the most dissatisfied and angry callers. If his team members couldn't resolve an issue, it escalated to him. That meant the people he spoke with were even more frustrated and unwilling to settle for any of the solutions offered. Sometimes they yelled. Other times they called him names. However, he was able to resolve most issues without escalating to his director for a refund.

Even though he could do the job, I knew he was miserable. Was this all there was in his future, working for low wages at a job he hated? How long could he do it?

I thought about my job delivering bread. The wonderful smells. Knowing I was feeding people. It was a satisfying way to make a living even if it didn't pay much.

Jose was spending more time with Sofia. Some nights he stayed with her rather than go home. Christian was working as much as he could. Sam stayed in the house most weekends, afraid to go out. The violence continued. Jose had reported he saw a dead body on the side of the road and assumed it was a gang killing.

The following Monday morning, Sam waited at the bus stop for an hour before walking back down the street. There was no bus. The news reported that the bus drivers had gone on strike, protesting the violence.

For two weeks, there was no public transportation. Sam and Jose called work, letting them know they had no way to get there. Their bosses asked them to take a cab to work. They also cut them down to two days a week but told them they'd have to work 16-hour shifts.

It was difficult to get a cab and the cost had increased because of the danger and high demand, but having the same schedule allowed the boys to share the fare.

With fewer overall hours, they were nervous about paying the bills. To make matters worse, Christian was laid off from his job. Due to the current situation, workers at the tire factory were also afraid to commute to work, so the plant decided to shut down until the crisis was resolved.

The boys stayed in the house. It wasn't safe outside. Violence was escalating and gangs controlled the streets. At night, they could hear gunshots and car horns. It seemed like chaos.

One evening, Sam called Brian and Marlene and opened up about what was going on. Even in Chicago, stories of the violence in El Salvador were in the news. They offered to help the boys with their rent until they could go back to work full-time.

"You are so lucky to have them," Jose said.

Jose came home one evening with news about *ex-pequeños*, boys they knew who had died in the gang violence. Boris, who had stayed with the Byrnes in Chicago during one of NPH's fiestas, was shot in the back during a gang raid. Brian and Marlene would be sad to hear that he had succumbed to the violence. So many NPH kids became lost when they left the safety of the home. They didn't have anyone to fall back on, and the gang "family" became their best, or only, option.

Sam and Jose continued to work double shifts but remained on high alert. Beyond the financial benefit, sharing a cab felt safer than being alone on the streets.

Christian was eventually called back to work. His schedule was random, and one Friday he left the tire plant late. He waited for a bus because he didn't want to spend what little money he had on a cab.

As he stood at the bus stop, three guys jumped out of a car to mug him. They were either angry because he had so little money or maybe he was just an easy target, regardless, they beat him bloody.

Jose and Sam were at home when a police car pulled up. The officer said they found him lying at the bus stop, unconscious. He was taken to the emergency room and cleaned up but would not stay because he didn't have the money to pay a hospital bill. So, the officer took his statement and drove him home. Christian had tried to remember the men, what kind of car, and what direction they came from, but it had all happened so fast.

Jose thanked the officer as Sam grabbed him around the waist to walk him inside. He was worse than they thought once they got him out of the shower. Bruises and cuts everywhere. The gang members had taken his wallet and his key to the tire factory.

"My boss will be mad that I lost that key," he said, his voice weak and pained.

The boys got him to eat and put him to bed. Jose kept an eye on him all night. Sam went to his room and stared at the ceiling, wide awake.

I was afraid of what was happening. I was sure Sam was too. We both had vivid memories of our delivery truck robbery. Was it only a matter of time before it happened to him again?

41

Murphy
Sam

IN THE FOLLOWING WEEKS, it became clear. There was no future, no family in El Salvador. I had made a mistake. Had I lost my chance at having a big dream?

I was calm and sure as I hit send on the email. Then, I just stared at the screen as if I expected an immediate response. It was easier to send an email request to Mel, Mary Jo, Brian, and Marlene than call.

I wanted to go back to Chicago. I wanted a second chance. I wanted to have a dream.

I asked to return to school and continue studying for my degree at Northeastern. I promised I was ready to complete my classwork. I had made a mistake by leaving. For two days, I waited, checking my email constantly.

The response came from Mary Jo, which surprised me.

She wrote, "I am answering because Marlene and Brian had to put Murphy down. He was sick and the vet said there was nothing they could do. He was in pain . . ."

I couldn't read on. I was crying. No, I was sobbing. Maybe not just for Murphy but for everything he represented. My old life with the Byrnes and with Murphy was over. I would never see him again. Never have him greet me at the front door. Never put my face in his soft fur.

It took a long time before I could read on.

"Of course, we can explore your return to study. Marlene and I will talk to the school and see about your student visa. We miss you and love you. We can't wait to see you and hear all about your time in El Salvador."

It had been almost a year since I left Chicago. So much had happened. Eva. Work. Violence. Murphy.

So much had changed. And I had changed.

On Saturday, Marlene and Brian FaceTimed me. I could see they were both sad about Murphy. Marlene remembered that she had promised he would be there when I came for a visit.

"Sam, I'm so sorry Murphy didn't make it. He won't be here if you return," she said. "We were devastated when the vet gave us the news."

I wanted to console her, but I couldn't. It was hard enough to hold back my own tears.

Brian changed the subject. "We talked to the school and requested they reinstate your student visa. They are not sure it can be ready by next semester, but they will try."

My heart jumped; my plan might work! I was ready.

"Thank you," was all I said, again holding back tears. This time, they were tears of joy.

"You need to continue working until we confirm the timing and your start date," Brian said. "It might be six months if we can't get you enrolled for the January semester."

I knew I could not be a legal student in the U.S. without official enrollment in classes. I would have to wait until my visa was approved.

Marlene noticed I was quiet, "Sam, are you okay?"

"Yes," I said. "I just want to try again and get a degree."

There was no way I was going to tell them all the stories about what had happened. That could wait until I was back in Chicago. Back "home."

For the next two weeks, I was anxious, jumpy at home, bouncing my foot at work, and unable to sleep at night. I did not want to tell Jose or Christian about my plan. I couldn't tell work I was quitting. It felt like it was right there in front of me, but so far out of reach.

The news came on a Friday. Marlene had secured the visa, and I was able to enroll in classes that started on January 6. She was excited about planning my return.

I decided to spend Christmas with Jose and Christian. I would tell them after the holiday. I rehearsed my speech every night. It would be hard, but I knew they would be happy for me.

Marlene scheduled my return flight for New Year's Eve to arrive just before midnight. A new year and a fresh start.

42

Goodbye
Jorge

I KNEW IT WAS OVER.

Sam quit his job. He informed his friends and gave them money for his share of the rent. He packed everything in his room. He said his goodbyes. Even as he drove to the airport, he never looked back. There was no hesitation.

Sam was heading to his new life. And this time, it was goodbye forever. Yet, I felt happy. I had watched him and, hopefully, helped guide him through some tough times from afar. Now, it was time for me to be in a better place, and more importantly, it was time for Sam to move on; pursue his dream.

The memories came flooding back to me. Finding him in the trash. His little hand sticking up. The blue blanket. The first time I handed him over to Rosa. Her warm, caring touch as she washed his dirty little body. Sam running to get the doors for me as I delivered bread. His quiet manner as we drove the delivery route. His ability to fade into the background when we had a new baby. Juggling for my girls. I felt a deep sense of loss.

I didn't need to look after him anymore. My job was finished. Sam had found his forever family. Brian and Marlene would be there for him. From now on, they would make sure he was safe. They would make him their own. In my heart, I knew he would never return to El Salvador.

I watched from my spot in the airport, waiting for it. Wanting him to sense my presence or my farewell. I knew it was our final goodbye.

He never looked back.

It was simply over.

43

Happy New Year

Sam

EVERYTHING SEEMED FAMILIAR AS I walked through O'Hare airport after I landed. Wasn't I just here? The restaurants were the same. The people pushing their bags, going places, looked familiar. I rode down the escalator, and there they were. All of them. Mel and Mary Jo. Brian and Marlene. Matthew and Maggie.

They were older. Matthew was taller. Maggie too. But they looked perfect to me.

I walked out into the cold parking structure, listening to everyone talk at once. The banter made me happy. Stopping for one moment, I took a huge breath and held it before exhaling. There it was. The cloud of white. It felt invigorating. Cleansing. Safe.

We piled into the van, and Matthew and Maggie sat in the third row. I told them stories of my year. The job. The violence. The house.

Somewhere along the drive, Maggie leaned forward, "We have a surprise," she said.

"What is it?" I asked. It felt good to see her happy face.

I couldn't imagine what she was suggesting.

"Don't tell him," Matthew said. She kept quiet, and my anticipation grew all the way home.

In the driveway, I wanted to help Brian with my bags, but Matt and Maggie grabbed my hands and pulled me toward the house.

"Come with us," Maggie said. They were so excited.

"Go ahead," Brian said with a smile.

Instead of going through the front door, we went through the garage and mudroom into the family room. Matthew ran ahead, opening the metal door of a crate on the floor. There he was, a little black puppy with his tail wagging, running toward me.

I knelt as he jumped into my lap and licked my face. His fur was like velvet, soft and new. He moved so fast it was hard to catch him. I lifted him up and put his little furry body up to my face.

"Say hello to Riley!"

Epilogue 2023

SAMUEL JIMENEZ COREAS

Sam flew back to Chicago on December 31, 2015. He returned to his studies at Northeastern Illinois University. Luis Ortiz was still there and ready to help Sam reach his goals.

In his first semester, Sam volunteered at the El Salvadoran Consulate office. Within a year, the Consul General of El Salvador, who was managing the office in Chicago, offered Sam a job. It allowed Sam to work for his country and continue his studies in the evenings and on weekends.

Sam graduated with honors, receiving a bachelor's degree in social work from NEIU in 2020. While working for the El Salvador Consulate in Chicago, he met and married Diana. Today, Sam continues to support the efforts of NPH through its fundraising office in Chicago. He speaks to groups about how NPH saved him from a life of poverty.

BISHOP RON HICKS

Ron Hicks became involved with NPH after college, volunteering at the NPH Mexico home for one year. During this time, he fell in love with the NPH mission and answered a call to the priesthood. After being ordained, Father Hicks worked in parishes in the Archdiocese of Chicago. In 2005, he asked the Cardinal to grant him the opportunity to serve as the regional director of NPH in

Central America. For five years, he lived at the home in El Salvador and managed five Central American NPH homes.

In 2010, he returned to Chicago to continue his work in the Archdiocese of Chicago. On September 17, 2018, Father Hicks was ordained a Bishop by Cardinal Blasé J. Cupich and became the Vicar General of the Archdiocese of Chicago. As part of the ordination, he created a coat of arms that included a representation of his time at NPH and the children he served in Central America. He is currently the Bishop of the Diocese of Joliet, Illinois. Bishop Ron continues to support NPH and visits the homes regularly.

NPH

In 1954, Father William Wasson saved a 15-year-old boy who stole money from the collection box from being sentenced to jail. It was the beginning of *Nuestros Pequeños Hermanos* (NPH). Today, NPH operates residential care homes for vulnerable children in El Salvador, Bolivia, Dominican Republic, Guatemala, Haiti, Honduras, Nicaragua, Peru, and Mexico. Founded on his principle of unconditional love, NPH has raised more than 20,000 children, changing their lives and helping them become leaders in their own countries.

In a shifting world climate, countries look to NPH to reach out to communities with programs and services for those in need. NPH has expanded its services, offering schooling for nonresident children and supplying healthcare resources and countless other programs to more than 170,000 children and families living in poverty.

Thanks to the financial support of its loyal donor base, NPH continues to reach the underprivileged in Latin America and the Caribbean. Driven by the core principles of founder Father William Wasson, NPH has a reputation for quality care and creates a culture of family both inside and outside its homes.

Support for NPH means an opportunity to break the cycle of poverty. It means raising leaders in their own countries who will affect their communities far into the future. It means NPH can offer community services to reach those in desperate need.

HOW TO DONATE:
NPH USA
134 North LaSalle Street
Suite 500
Chicago, IL 60602-1036

www.nphusa.org
888–201-8880

Book Club Discussion
For *Do Not Discard*

These discussion ideas are meant to enhance your book club experience. The questions should spur new and interesting angles and topics for discussion about the story and how each reader can learn from Sam to change the world. We hope the ideas enrich your conversation and increase the enjoyment of sharing a good story together.

1. *He was always trying to stay one step ahead of any banditos on our route from store to store. He showed me how to remove the sole of my shoe and create a small, secure space, wrapping things in paper so as not to make any noise when I walked. He even gave me coins to practice with.*

We all have little secrets passed down by our family members. Jorge wanted to protect Sam. Did your family have secret hiding spots, little traditions, or special lessons that kept you safe? If so, did you pass them down to your family?

2. *As we drove on, she became smaller and smaller until she was out of sight. In my dream, I looked over at Jorge. He was happily whistling*

a song. It was strange since I had never seen him do anything like that. I hoped he would talk to me, but he didn't. He just kept looking straight ahead, as if the baby and I didn't exist.

I looked down at the baby quietly resting in my arms. His dark eyes stared up at me as if he knew I would care for him and keep him safe. He had dirt on his forehead and cheek. I wiped it away. Jorge reached over and began rubbing the baby's forearm, touching it softly, like he was afraid he might hurt him if he pressed too hard.

Sam dreams about his mother and pictures himself as a baby. What does it mean that Sam's mother is in his dreams? Can we create a presence for those we never have met and don't know? Can we forgive those who hurt us? Do we need to in order to move on with our lives?

3. *Jose didn't talk the rest of the way. He just stared straight ahead and kept moving. I walked with my head high and my heart beating out of my chest. Freedom makes you feel like a man. There is no one telling you what to do. No chores. No bells ringing to tell you to eat. I knew the street would be hard but, at least—and for the first time in my life—I was in control.*

When is the first time you felt in control of your life? What makes you feel free? Are there things we take for granted? Have there been moments when you have "run" from life and found the feeling of freedom?

4. *The founder of NPH, Father William Wasson, was scheduled to visit and the place was buzzing, anticipating his arrival from Mexico. Things were being painted and cleaned. Father Ron's Saturday evening sermons were themed around the good works of Father Wasson, including the story of how he started NPH in Mexico. The older kids told their own stories about him to the new kids who had never met him. The reverence for this priest, the one*

responsible for their home, and the understanding of his core principles were clear to the kids, the staff, and the volunteers.

Have you met your idol? What qualities does someone need to be revered? Do we spend too much time idolizing people for the wrong reasons? What actions of those we respect should we emulate?

5. *Sam and Maggie sat down to watch Funniest Home Videos. Tonight, she climbed on the back of the couch with the remote, sitting on his shoulder. The show started, and they were soon laughing loudly. One video showed a dog covered in mud and hiding from his owners. Another featured a baby spitting out vegetables. Next, a cat was falling into a pool, and then a baby could not stop laughing. All of it made them both join in.*

Sometimes it's the simple things that unite us. What can we do to understand each other? How do we work to make connections with people who are different from us? Are our hearts open?

6. *"I know you are scared. This is big," I said. He didn't say anything. "Just remember, you are a good musician. Your songs are great, people love you, and the musicians playing with you have your back. I've watched you from the beginning, at practice, at NPH, and even here in the house. More than anyone, I know you can do this."*

Simple acts of kindness. How much do they impact the people around us? How often do we hand out compliments, encouragement, and kind words? Could we try to do more good? Does doing good make us feel better?

7. *On the first day, I barely caught a glimpse of him, but each day after, I noticed something new about him. He had a cover to protect his things on rainy days. He kept his water bottle in the same place on the cement ledge. There was a book next to it. He reminded me of*

the days I had lived under the bridge. I wondered where those guys were now. Could they still be living on the streets? Was someone new occupying my spot under our bridge? What had happened to the few items I had left behind?

Does Sam feel more connection to the homeless man than his peers? Does he help us realize how we judge from a distance? Does he make us reconsider our norms in life?

8. *As they replayed the house tour with the woman, they started to see the clues. "Why didn't we notice the door was wide open?" Jose asked, under his breath. "She never used a key to get in." "She must have broken in before we arrived," Sam said. "Why didn't we get her name and ask for identification?" Sam looked down at his granola bar and said, "I'll call Marlene and Brian."*

Who do we turn to in times of need? Do we appreciate the people in our lives that are our foundation? When does Sam come to understand he has a family? Is this why Jorge disappears?

9. *He said his goodbyes. Even as he drove to the airport, he never looked back. There was no hesitation. Sam was heading to his new life. And this time, it was goodbye forever. Yet, I felt happy. I had watched him and, hopefully, helped guide him through some tough times from afar.*

What is the significance of Jorge staying in El Salvador? What emotions do you think he is expressing? What emotions have changed for Sam? Is there a time when you know you have moved on from something and it feels good?

Do Not Discard

We hope you enjoyed the story of Samuel and it inspires you to reach for your dreams. Please share the book with friends, family, and colleagues. As a small publisher, we count on readers to be ambassadors for our authors.

We hope you will take the time to share your comments about Sam's story with other readers or post a review online.

Our authors love to meet with fans and enjoy taking time to talk with them about their stories. If you have a book club or would like to schedule a reading, we would love to hear from you. To contact us or for other releases and news about us, visit www.goodstoriespublishing.com.

If you liked *DO NOT DISCARD* and want to hear more of the story, you can read Juan's journey in Marlene's book *MUSIC HAS LEGS*. Juan's story showcases his rise from the streets of El Salvador to playing the drums at NPH to recording his music and playing on stage in Chicago. Check out the book on Amazon.

About The Author

MARLENE FARRELL BYRNE

Marlene has been writing her entire life for both fun and work. She began writing full-time after leaving her position as CEO of Celtic Chicago, a full-service branding and marketing agency. Throughout her life, she balanced motherhood and career while giving time to important causes such as NPH.

Her charity work led her to the Board of Directors for NPH USA, where she accepted the opportunity to care for Juan Manuel Pineda, leading her to meet and become family to Samuel. His story inspired her to write *Do Not Discard*.

Marlene and her husband, Brian, have three children: Matthew, Maggie, and Samuel, and a dog named Riley.

Other Books by Marlene Byrne

Change the World. Start with the Children: A Book That Directly Supports Nuestros Pequeños Hermanos Homes is about Father William Wasson, the priest who founded Nuestros Pequeños Hermanos homes for orphaned and vulnerable children.

Music Has Legs is the inspirational story about Juan Manuel Pineda and what people are capable of when they come together for good. www.goodstoriespublishing.com

Project Play Children's Books series, including *Kick the Can, Treasure Hunt, Ghost in the Graveyard, Follow the Leader,* and *Just a Baseball Game.* www.projectplaybooks.com

All books are available on Amazon.com.